THE LEGAL IMPLICATIONS OF SELF-DEFENSE

THE LEGAL IMPLICATIONS OF SELF-DEFENSE

A Reference Manual for The Martial Arts

GERALD M. WALSTON

VANTAGE PRESS

New York Washington Atlanta Hollywood

FIRST EDITION

Published by Vantage Press, Inc.
516 West 34th Street, New York, New York 10001

Manufactured in the United States of America
Standard Book Number 533-03539-2

CONTENTS

PART IV—LEGAL IMPLICATIONS FOR THE SCHOOL AND INSTRUCTOR

PART V—SELECTING A LAWYER

LIST OF FIGURES

ACKNOWLEDGMENTS

The author expresses his deep appreciation to Aytac Bozkurt and Jairo Gomez for drafting the illustrations and to Shirley Jacob for her assistance in typing part of the manuscript.

INTRODUCTION

With the rapid spread of the martial arts in the United States today, many people are acquiring the means to physically injure others, either temporarily or permanently. The person who misuses this new found ability can become invovled in serious legal difficulty due to civil lawsuit and/or criminal proceedings. Such legal entanglements can be very costly and result in imprisonment as well.

This is a book about law as it affects the use of self-defense in the United States. It is an attempt by the author to make the topic both easily understandable as well as comprehensive. The author noticed a widespread ignorance of the legal implications of using martial arts techniques in actual fighting situations on the part of both instructors and students. The author's search for a legal understanding revealed the complete lack of a readily understandable in-depth text, oriented specifically toward the martial arts. Undoubtedly the absence of such a text to date is due to the complexity of the topic and to the fact that each state has its own wording for its laws, no two states having the same wording. To have included a reference to the laws of each state for each subject discussed would have resulted in an oversized book of considerably higher cost. The author believes the generalized discussion format followed fits within the intent of the laws of every state.

The essential point to be made is that misuse of martial arts techniques can lead to criminal charges and/or civil lawsuit. The legal framework of American society generally opposes the use of physical force against another person unless absolutely necessary to prevent physical injury to the defender. This use of force for defensive purposes is granted to all citizens by the United States Constitution whether or not they have martial arts training.

Very few instructors in the martial arts are lawyers. It is also rare for an instructor to thoroughly research the law and inform students as to when a person may be physically struck in the name of self-defense. Unfortunately most instructors teach only the physical techniques of self-defense, which can be dangerous for the student from a legal standpoint. This book attempts to fill the gap by explaining the legal uses of these physical techniques. As of this writing, no other book provides such a comprehensive viewpoint for the benefit of all martial arts students and instructors. The author has kept the language of the text as simple as possible and has assumed that the reader has no background whatsoever in law. Wherever possible, the various legal procedures have been diagrammed to make the overall presentation more easily understandable.

Self-defense, in the legal sense, as used in this book, is the legal right of an individual to protect himself from criminal or civil wrong. This defense may involve the use of force, but not necessarily. The average martial arts student may have a vague idea as to when he can use his techniques for defense—but this notion may be incorrect under the law. What is worse, however, is that very few students have any idea of the legal consequences for misusing the techniques of self-defense.

Consequently, the book is basically comprised of five parts. The first part discusses what the law consists of and under what circumstances one may legally use force for self-defense. The author has attempted to explain in simple and understandable language the various crimes one might become involved in when physically attempting to strike or actually striking another person. Numerous examples related to the martial arts are included.

Part II outlines the criminal legal procedures you may encounter should you misuse your techniques. These are the various legal steps which the city, state, or federal government may take against you and the procedures that occur in criminal court.

The author's viewpoint is that it is not enough for martial arts students to know under what circumstances one may physically strike another person as self-defense (Part 1 of the book). The law is very complex. What you interpret as a situation constituting self-defense on your part, may be interpreted otherwise by a police officer or by the person you strike. In fact you may be innocent, having acted justifiably under the law. This does not mean, however, that criminal charges will not be brought against you.

Part III discusses what you may expect if a civil lawsuit is filed against you. Part Two is concerned with the action that a government might take against you for committing a crime whereas Part Three discusses what actions an injured person may take against you to compensate for injuries.

Part IV of the book is valuable for the instructor of a self-defense or martial arts school. The legal implications of teaching physical techniques are discussed. Under some circumstances, a student who is injured in class could file a civil lawsuit against the instructor. The author points out some of those situations and provides suggestions for avoiding such situations.

Part V discusses finding a lawyer and what the cost will be to you should professional legal aid be necessary. It is hoped that the reader will become aware of the legal restrictions for all martial arts practitioners regarding the use of physical techniques. It is hoped that by providing a full view of the law and court procedures you can avoid legal problems involving misuse of the techniques of a particular martial art whether it is Taekwon-Do, Karate, Kung-Fu, Judo, etc. It is the intention of the author to expose martial arts students to some of the technicalities of the law, in regard to self-defense, so that each student will develop a stronger sense of moral responsibility.

At the end of the book is a glossary that defines the more important terms used in the book. To allow readers to easily locate a given topic of interest, an index is also provided.

It seems clear that it is the moral obligation of all martial arts instructors to both understand and explain to their students the legal implications of self-defense. Further, it becomes the moral responsibility of all martial arts students to use their techniques within the legal guidelines of our social system. This book has attempted to explain these guidelines.

The author welcomes any comments or suggestions from readers of this text. Particularly appreciated would be references to any actual cases involving some legal aspect of the martial arts.

Gerald Walston
43 Cross Road
Morris Plains
New Jersey 07950

THE LEGAL IMPLICATIONS OF SELF-DEFENSE

Part I

THE LAW

Chapter 1

CONCEPT OF LAW

Before proceeding into a discussion of various crimes, criminal court procedures, and civil court procedures, it is necessary to define what law is. At the same time, it will be helpful to briefly explain how law originated and developed into its present form in the United States. Finally, the topic of crime versus civil wrongs is examined.

DEFINITION OF LAW

The logical beginning point in a discussion concerning a topic of law is to define the concept of law. In our day-to-day conversations, we may use the word *law* in several ways. For example, there are the laws of nature, Newton's law of gravity, the laws of economics, the laws of God, etc. However, these are not the kinds of laws pertinent to this text.

A law, as we are to use the term, is a rule of human conduct or action that either has been established by custom or else has been legislated into being by an authorized group. This rule may be enforced by a governing body, such as a city, a state, or a nation. Thus the kind of law with which we will be concerned owes its existence to organized human society. Law, as we are discussing it, could not exist in primitive societies. Admittedly, primitive societies do operate under systems of taboos and tribal customs, but these taboos and customs are not organized nor written nor are they voted into existence.

SOURCES OF LAW

To develop an understanding of why the law is so complex, let us consider a brief synopsis of the historical origins of law. The earliest source of law was undoubtedly custom, similar to the customs and taboos present today in primitive cultures. Early custom was oral and applied to familial interactions and to the small nomadic hunting groups composed of several families. These early customs were probably either religious or functional in nature. As these groups developed from hunting into agrarian, or farming, societies, a more complex organization of society was necessitated. Initially, the earlier customs comprised the law. With more complex interactions occurring among people, more customs were established. The body of law which is based on custom is known as the *common law.*

Common law, which developed in England, came to America with the Pilgrims in the seventeenth century. Once permanency was established in America by the early settlers, customs necessarily began to vary from those in England. Thus today we see that the common law is not the same in content as that in England although both sets of present day law have a common base. In fact, common law varies from state to state within the United States.

However, not all present day law in the United States originated with English common law. For example, Louisiana was the only state that did not originally follow the common law. Rather, Louisiana was under the *civil law* due to the influence of its French and Spanish founders. (Civil law, as used here, differs from civil, or tort, law as discussed later.) Civil law is much older than common law, having originated in the Roman Empire. When English common law was first being written (as opposed to oral preservation) in the early seventh century, Roman civil law was already a well-developed system of human conduct that superbly suited the advanced and progressive Roman society. Subsequent to the fall of the Roman Empire, civil law was enhanced with the addition of the French Naploeonic code, another system of law, which also had a Roman origin. Generally speaking, all of continental Europe owes its present day law system to the Romans. In 1805, Louisiana adopted the English common law for its criminal law. Today each of the United States thus follows the English common law.

To summarize, there are two important origins of present day law. First, the civil law, present in continental Europe and the State of Louisiana in the past, originated in the Roman Empire. Second, the common law, present in England and the United States, originated in England.

One important aspect of English common law separating it from Roman civil law is the concept of *trial by jury,* which originated under common law. In any jury trial, the task of the jury is to determine facts. Lawyers bring in witnesses and experts to a trial to testify before the jury so that the jury can assemble a body of fact substantial enough to decide on the guilt or innocence of the defending party. The judge is present at a jury trial in order to interpret the law as it pertains to the case for the benefit of the jury. Thus at a trial, the jury determines fact, the judge determines law, and lawyers offer facts to the jury in favor of their client.

As a historical insight, the jury trial concept was introduced into England as a result of the Norman conquest in 1066. The new administrators (the dukes of Normandy) introduced a system whereby persons answered, under oath, questions concerning tax revenues. The system gradually began to be used in civil cases, and by 1300 the jury was in widespread use throughout England.

A second aspect distinguishing English common law from Roman civil law is the common law doctrine of *precedent.* Under this doctrine, the courts accumulate the written decisions of each case. Further, the courts tend to follow the principles decided in previous cases. In other words, the courts follow precedent. This, in effect, gives some predictability to the common law, provided one knows the principles of common law related to the case at hand. In the United States, this is known as the principle of *stare decisis*. This principle did not exist under Roman law. Instead, each specific situation requiring legal decision was incorporated into the Civil Code, a monstrous set of volumes containing all Roman law.

A third form of law, the most recently developed form, is *statutory law*. It is a highly organized body of law that has come into being through the legislative process of organized society. The word "statute" means "law." The federal government passes federal statutes and states pass state statutes. Smaller governmental bodies, such as cities, pass laws called *ordinances*. The collection of federal or state statutes or city ordinances into a comprehensive reference is called a *code*. There are both civil and criminal codes for these governmental levels. Any new statute or ordinance passed by these bodies produces a change in the code. Old and outdated laws also may be repealed by these governmental units. Thus the codes are not permanent or unchanging. They gradually change with time and the addition of new statutes and ordinances. As a result, the codes may be said to reflect the social status of the times.

The basis on which these various governmental units may either pass or repeal laws is set by federal and state constitutions. These constitutions declare which branch of the government may pass and repeal laws and which branch will be responsible for enforcing these laws. They also define the procedure that must be followed in order to enact a new law.

The United States Constitution, originated in 1788, is the highest governing law in the United States. Federal law, under the United States Constitution, takes precedence over any and all state laws. In other words, no state may pass a law that conflicts with or replaces any federal statute. Likewise, no city ordinance can take precedence over its state's laws.

CRIMES VERSUS TORTS

Now that the reader has a basic understanding of how present day law originated and how new laws may be created, let us examine the two major fields of law—*crimes* and *torts*. An individual may commit two general classes of wrongs under the American legal system, hence American law has two fields of law dealing with these two types of wrongs.

CRIMES

A crime is a wrong committed against a state or the United States. Such a wrong violates specific laws and is punishable by a fine and/or imprisonment. The section on specific crimes will discuss in detail various crimes that have some relationship to the martial arts either directly or indirectly. The section on criminal court procedure will outline the steps that you may expect to occur should you ever be involved in a criminal court trial or should you be arrested as a suspect in a crime. Some of the crimes discussed include the various categories of homicide, assault, battery, mayhem, and disturbing the peace.

When a crime is committed, there are two parties involved. One is the victim of the crime and the other is the committer of the crime. The victim is referred to as the *plaintiff*, i.e. the one who has suffered a wrong. The committer of the crime is referred to as the *defendant*, i.e. the one who must defend himself (with a lawyer's professional assistance) from the criminal charges. In all criminal cases, the plaintiff is the state (or city or federal government).

Crimes are divided into two basic types:

1. *Felonies.* A felony is a serious crime such as murder, robbery, arson, and rape, which can be punished either with death or a prison term (state or federal prison). Felonies are prosecuted in state or federal courts.
2. *Misdemeanors.* A misdemeanor is any illegal offense less serious than a felony, which can be punished with a fine and/or a jail term. Misdemeanors are prosecuted in county or municipal courts.

TORTS

A tort is a wrong committed against an individual. Punishment for this wrong usually consists of the court requiring the guilty person (the defendant) to pay the wronged person (the plaintiff) damages. Such cases are tried in civil courts rather than in criminal courts. (These civil courts and civil laws are not related to the Roman civil law discussed earlier. The word "civil" is an unfortunate coincidence.) Thus one found guilty in a civil court of having committed a tort cannot be fined or sentenced to jail or prison as in criminal court. Instead, the civil court can order the guilty person to pay for whatever damage or injuries the illegal act may have caused. Such a payment is referred to as *damages*.

The section on torts discusses the types of civil wrongs that students of the martial arts might be involved with. The section on civil court procedure explains what steps you may expect to occur should you be involved in a civil lawsuit.

Chapter 2

REQUIREMENTS FOR CRIME

There are several requirements to be fulfilled in order for a crime to be existent. First, there must be criminal intent present. Second, there must be a criminal act in conjunction with the intent. Third, the person committing the act must be of a required statutory age in order to be held liable for the crime.

CRIMINAL INTENT

Criminal intent is referred to as the *mens rea* in the legal profession. This is a Latin phrase generally meaning intent. In order to mentally develop criminal intent, you must have legal mental capacity. Consequently, a legally insane person is not considered able to develop criminal intent, and thus you sometimes hear of a plea of insanity in a criminal case. The defendant is claiming that he was incapable of distinguishing right from wrong at the time of the crime and, therefore, could not have developed intent.

However, the law does not allow a person who is legally sane but voluntarily under the influence of drugs or alcohol a defense from having criminal intent for that reason. In effect, the law says that if you are legally sane, then you will be held responsible for any criminal acts you might commit while affected by drugs or alcohol.

In most cases, a defendant's true intent will not be known as he will not have declared his intent before, during, or after the crime. However, the law says that a person's actions indicate intent.

Suppose an unarmed attacker on the street attempts to punch you. In defending yourself, you kick the attacker in the head and break his neck thereby killing him. Even though you did not intend to kill the attacker, the court will judge your intent according to your actions. The court will probably claim that you should have known what the consequences would be if you kicked someone in the head very strongly.

As another example, imagine that John is in a bar. He drinks too much while there. Being a black belt, he attempts to prove his ability to a friend by kicking holes in the wall. Even though John is under the influence of alcohol, he will be held criminally liable for his intent.

Let us say that you are at a friend's house. His young son puts his father's tool box in your car without your knowledge. It is not until the next day that you find the tool box and return it. The law would say that, in this case, no intent for taking the box was present on your part; therefore, no theft could be charged against you.

CRIMINAL ACT

Intent alone does not constitute a crime. There must also be a criminal act associated with the intent. The law defines what these various acts are. The acts of particular interest to the students of martial arts are described in the section on specific crimes.

AGE REQUIREMENT

Figure I-1 shows by both state and sex the oldest age at which juvenile courts have jurisdiction over youths having com-

FIGURE I–1

Age at Which Juvenile or Adult Criminal Laws Apply

State	Oldest Age of Which Juvenile Courts Have Juris-diction		Youngest Age at Which Adult Courts Have Jurisdiction	
	Male	Female	Male	Female
Alabama	15	15	16	16
Alaska*	17–20	17–20	18–21	18–21
Arizona	17	17	18	18
Arkansas	17	17	18	18
California	20	20	21	21
Colorado*	16–20	16–20	17–21	17–21
Connecticut	15	15	16	16
Delaware*	17–20	17–20	18–21	18–21
District of Columbia*	18–21	17–20	17–20	18–21
Florida*	16–20	16–20	17–21	17–21
Georgia*	16–20	16–20	17–21	17–21
Hawaii	17	17	18	18
Idaho	17	17	18	18
Illinois*	16–20	17–20	17–21	18–21
Indiana*	17–20	17–20	18–21	18–21
Iowa	17	17	18	18
Kansas	15	17	16	18
Kentucky	17	17	18	18
Louisiana	16	16	17	17
Maine	16	16	17	17
Maryland	17	17	18	18
Massachusetts*	16–17	16–17	17–18	17–18
Michigan*	16–18	16–18	17–19	17–19
Minnesota	17	17	18	18
Mississippi*	16–19	16–19	17–20	17–20
Missouri*	17–20	17–20	18–21	18–21
Montana	17	17	18	18
Nebraska	17	17	18	18
Nevada*	17–20	17–20	18–21	18–21
New Hampshire*	17–20	17–20	18–21	18–21
New Jersey	17	17	18	18
New Mexico*	17–20	17–20	18–21	18–21
New York	15	17	16	18
North Carolina	15	15	16	16
North Dakota	17	17	18	18
Ohio*	17–20	17–20	18–21	18–21
Oklahoma	15	17	16	18
Oregon*	17–20	17–20	18–21	18–21

FIGURE I–1 Cont'd

Age At Which Juvenile or Adult Criminal Laws Apply

State	Oldest Age at Which Juvenile Courts Have Jurisdiction		Youngest Age at Which Adult Courts Have Jurisdiction	
	Male	**Female**	**Male**	**Female**
Pennsylvania*	17–20	17–20	18–21	18–21
Rhode Island*	17–20	17–20	18–21	18–21
South Carolina*	16–20	16–20	17–21	17–21
South Dakota	17	17	18	18
Tennessee*	17–20	17–20	18–21	18–21
Texas*	16–20	17–20	17–21	18–21
Utah*	17–20	17–20	18–21	18–21
Vermont*	15–20	15–20	16–21	16–21
Virginia*	17–20	17–20	18–21	18–21
Washington*	17–20	17–20	18–21	18–21
West Virginia*	17–20	17–20	18–21	18–21
Wisconsin	17	17	18	18
Wyoming*	17–20	17–20	18–21	18–21

**NOTE:* These states allow the juvenile court to retain jurisdiction over the juvenile through and including the older age given in the juvenile columns if, at the younger age given, the juvenile is under the juvenile court's jurisdiction for having committed an offense.

mitted crimes. Also Figure I–1 shows by state and sex the youngest age at which adult criminal courts can have jurisdiction over youths committing criminal offenses. Notice that in some states there is an overlapping range of years over which either juvenile or adult court jurisdiction may occur. This apparent overlap occurs because these states allow a juvenile who has committed an offense and is under the court's jurisdiction when the maximum age is reached to remain under the juvenile court's jurisdiction either until his probation or reformatory term expires or until the maximum age of the overlap range is reached.

For example, suppose John, a martial arts student, commits severe battery against another person without any provocation. Since he is a resident of Colorado and is fifteen years old, he cannot be charged in an adult criminal court with having committed battery. Rather, he is brought into juvenile court. Due to the severity of the battery, he is placed on probation for three years. In Colorado, normally upon reaching the age of seventeen adult criminal courts have jurisdiction. However, John's juvenile probation does not expire until age eighteen. Therefore he remains under juvenile court jurisdiction until the probation expires when he is in his eighteenth year.

Chapter 3

SPECIFIC CRIMES

Having essentially defined what a crime is and who may commit a crime, we now proceed to the section that may be of greatest interest to most readers—the discussion of specific crimes. This book is not intended to be a complete text on all crimes and is limited to crimes applicable to the martial arts and to physical self-defense. Thus not all categories of crime are discussed, but only those crimes which a martial arts student might be directly involved with through use or misuse of his techniques. (See Figure I–2.)

Further, it should be kept in mind that the discussion is from a general point of view as there are differences in laws and definitions from state to state. For specific details on the laws or definitions of specific crimes in your state, you should consult an attorney. It cannot be emphasized too strongly that should you become involved in a crime or should you be charged with committing a crime, whether guilty or innocent, obtain the services of an attorney as soon as possible. The reason for this will become much clearer in later discussions of criminal and civil court procedures.

It is the intent of this section to fully educate the reader on the crimes he may most likely face that involve defensive situations. It is hoped that this educational objective accomplishes two purposes. First, the reader, by understanding what actions consti-

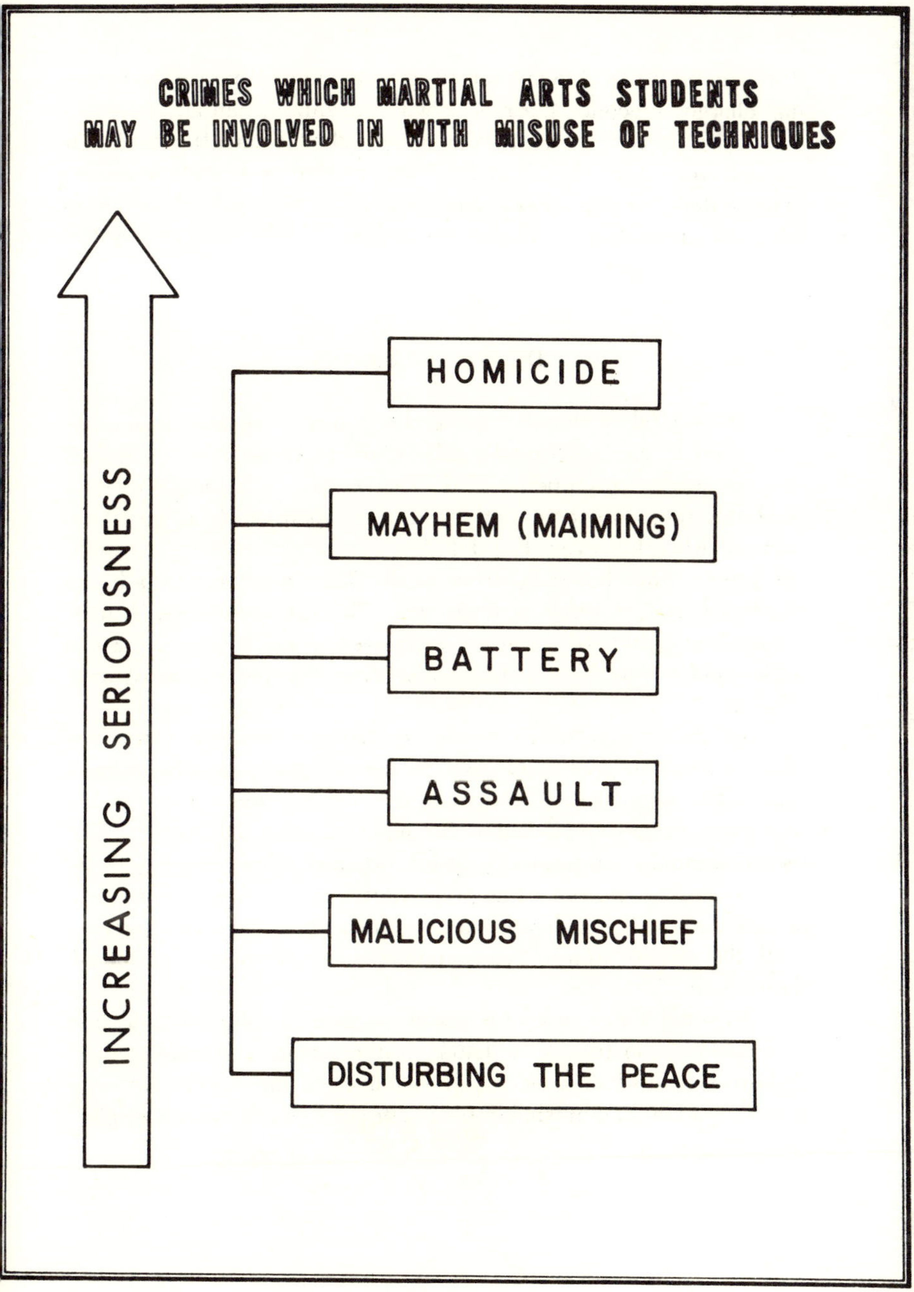
CRIMES WHICH MARTIAL ARTS STUDENTS
MAY BE INVOLVED IN WITH MISUSE OF TECHNIQUES
INCREASING SERIOUSNESS
HOMICIDE
MAYHEM (MAIMING)
BATTERY
ASSAULT
MALICIOUS MISCHIEF
DISTURBING THE PEACE

FIGURE I–2

tute the crime, will avoid acting so as to subject himself to criminal charges. Second, the reader will recognize when an adversary or a third party is committing a crime either toward the reader or toward someone else. Further, the reader will understand to what extent he may reasonably proceed to use his techniques to stop the crime from being committed, or whether use of physical techniques is even justified.

DEADLY WEAPON

In general, it may be stated that a deadly weapon is any object used to cause serious bodily injury or death. Such a definition is deliberately open-ended. That is, the definition obviously includes the more commonly known weapons such as guns and knives. Also, however, the definition includes anything else used to cause serious bodily harm or death. This could include a bat, a broken bottle, a brick, a chair, etc. The list is endless. A nunchaku, very obviously, can be considered a deadly weapon. Some cities and towns have laws against even the possession of nunchakus.

Of great importance to the martial arts student is the fact that a hand or foot may also be considered a deadly weapon under this definition. In this case, it is not the object that the law considers dangerous; it is how the object is used. Obviously a foot is not normally considered a deadly weapon. However, if you severely injure a person using your martial arts kicking techniques, a jury may well decide that your trained ability to kick, together with the serious injury of your opponent, constitutes use of a deadly weapon.

In some states, use of a deadly weapon in committing assault or battery constitutes a felony rather than a misdemeanor. Whereas a misdemeanor is punishable by a fine and/or jail sentence, a felony is punishable by a state (or federal) prison term.

ASSAULT

SIMPLE ASSAULT

One of the most common situations a martial arts student may face involves the crime of assault. Assault is both a crime and a tort so that the following definition applies to both. The only difference between civil assault and criminal assault is the penalty for the offense and the court having jurisdiction to impose the penalty. Assault may be defined as an unlawful apparent attempt, by a person having the apparent ability, to commit a bodily injury on another person. This definition may be broken into four components:

1. A physical act must occur.
2. The act must be unlawful.
3. An apparent ability to commit bodily injury must be present.
4. An apparent attempt to commit bodily injury must be present.

First, any threatening physical act is sufficient to constitute assault. It is not possible for words alone to constitute assault, regardless of how threatening, insulting, abusive, or nasty the words are. Words without physical action do not create assault. For example, if I call you and every member of your family various foul things, no assault has been committed. If I threaten to get my club, and hit you if you don't leave, although I don't move when talking, no assault has been committed. If I threaten to punch or kick you but make no move to do so, no assault occurs. Assault requires the presence of a physical act, but it does not require any accompanying verbal threats. The act of pulling your fist back to punch may serve as sufficient threat to create fear in the other person's mind of your apparent intent to injure him.

Second, the physical act must be unlawful. Any attempt to physically strike a person without legal justification is unlawful.

For example, if I dislike you intensely, it is not legally justifiable for me to attempt to strike you simply because you are in my presence. Similarly, if you call me various repulsive things, that is not legal justification for me to attempt to strike you.

Third, there must be an apparent ability to commit bodily injury. As an extreme example, a ninety-year-old lady threatening to work over a 200-pound football player is absurd. There is a lack of ability on the old lady's part to do such a thing. However, if the situation is reversed and the big man threatens to work over the old lady, then there is an obvious apparent ability. If I call you on the telephone and threaten to strike you with my club, no assault has been committed. This is for the simple reason that I obviously cannot strike you without being in your presence. The requirement here is that there be an apparent ability to commit bodily injury. It is not necessary to have actual or real ability to cause bodily injury in order to commit assault. For example, if I aim a rifle at you and threaten to shoot, I have committed assault even though the rifle is not loaded. Of course, no assault is committed if you knew at the time that the rifle was not loaded.

Fourth, there must be an apparent attempt to commit bodily injury to constitute assault. Sometimes assault is defined as an attempted battery. It is this apparent attempt to injure that demonstrates the criminal intent of the act. Threatening to kick someone, while at the same time actually kicking at the person, but missing, constitutes assault. More generally, threatening to strike or injure a person in any manner and actually carrying through with the attempt but failing to make physical contact constitutes assault. Displaying a fake bomb to someone and threatening to detonate it constitutes assault if the other person believes the bomb is real.

This means, then, that you as a martial arts student should not threaten to use your techniques or threaten to strike another person in any manner regardless of the circumstances. If you create an apprehension or fear in that threatened person's mind that you may actually injure him, then you have committed assault. Whether or not you actually intended to injure the person is irrelevant. Once the victim detects your apparent ability, and hears your threat, he may interpret your movement as the apparent attempt to injure him. Aside from any moral issues, it would be a very rare circumstance to legally justify a threat coupled with an attempt to injure someone. This is in reference to you as the initiator of the action and the attempt without any legal provocation on the part of the other person.

AGGRAVATED ASSAULT

Aggravated assault is an assault committed with any weapon that might be considered deadly or dangerous. The beginning section for specific crimes defined what a deadly weapon is under the law. You should be aware that some states consider assault with a deadly weapon a felony rather than a misdemeanor. However, it seems very unlikely that a martial arts student would be charged with a felony for threatening to use a martial arts kick or hand strike on someone. It is much more probable that such a threat would be treated as simple assault, which is a misdemeanor. Nevertheless, the intelligent student should never threaten anyone with his techniques so as to put himself in jeopardy of being charged with criminal assault.

BATTERY

Battery is the unlawful contact made on a person by a voluntary physical act of the aggressor against the consent of the victim. Although many people consider battery to be a beating of some degree, in the legal sense the amount of force involved in the contact is immaterial.

The two basic components of battery are physical contact and unlawful force.

First, no matter how strong or weak the force is, if no physical contact is made then there is no battery committed. (This act, lacking actual contact, would be an assault.) The contact may be very slight as well as quite strong. Various examples of contact include:

1. Shoving, pushing, grabbing, or throwing a person.
2. Punching, kicking, or otherwise striking a person.
3. Touching a person's clothing that he is wearing but not necessarily touching his body.
4. Touching something he is carrying, such as a walking cane.
5. Spitting on someone.
6. Touching him with some object such as a rock, an arrow, a club.

Second, the physical contact must result from unlawful force. In effect, this component of the definition of battery is referring to the intent of the striker. As a result, the many day-to-day physical contacts we experience are not considered batteries because there is no criminal, or unlawful, intent involved in the contacts. For example, standing in a crowded elevator, in a crowded bus, or in a crowded subway car, you experience numerous contacts but since none are unlawful, then none are batteries. In these circumstances, you give implied consent for the public at large to bump into you or sit close to you on a crowded seat. Thus it may be said that a contact is unlawful if it was not consented to either expressly or impliedly.

On the other hand, if you are in the presence of someone whom you intensely dislike and, without legal justification, you begin a malicious shoving match, you have committed a battery with your first shove. Similarly, if you slap this person instead of shoving him, you again have committed a battery. If you spit in his face, this is a battery. If you throw a rock or bottle at him and strike him, this is a battery. It is battery if you strike him with any kind of weapon. Grabbing his coat by the lapel is a battery. The point to make note of here is that physical injury need not be present in order for a battery to have been committed.

Consider now what this means to you as a martial arts student. First, it means that you should never threaten anyone, particularly the kind of threat involving finger thumping on the other person's chest to make a point or grabbing a coat lapel, necktie, or arm. Threats of physical injury against other persons are not justifiable for any martial arts student either legally or morally.

Second, you should avoid initiating the physical contact in a fight with another person. For those occasions where it is necessary for your self-preservation for you to act first, both quickly and decisively, you must be certain of your legal justification for so acting. This will be discussed further in the section on self-defense.

Third, it is appropriate to make one interesting point concerning self-defense in regard to battery. Consider the situation where someone attempts to strike you without any justifiable provocation on your part, but misses. It looks obvious that the attacker intends to try to physically injure you, so you disable him in self-defense, with your defense being legally appropriate. At this point, you could charge your attacker with assault (not battery because he made no physical contact in his attempt to strike you), but he could not charge you with battery. Once a person begins an illegal attack on another person, the attacker loses his legal rights to protection from battery.

Fourth, if you are called vulgar names, or if repulsive references are made to members of your family, you must maintain your self-control and avoid striking or touching the name caller. His name calling is not illegal, but if you strike him, that is illegal as is any other physical contact with him which he has not consented to.

Fifth, in any martial arts competition, there can be no charging of battery by one participant against another if injury occurs. The law assumes that both competitors by their very presence in the ring granted consent to be struck. Competition of this nature is considered mutual combat with each participant accepting the risk for any injury to himself.

ASSAULT AND BATTERY

It is common to hear a person speak of "assault and battery" in reference to a physical attack as if a single law covered the topic. However, the previous discussions reveal that the occurrences of assault and battery are legally separable events. In many cases, though, if battery occurs, then in all likelihood, assault has also occurred. These cases occur when a threat is followed by actual physical contact. Remember that physical injury is not required in order for battery to have been committed.

Although it is more common for assault to occur alone as a single offense, it is possible for battery to occur alone. For example, if I sneak up behind you and hit you over the head with a stick, then I have committed battery but not assault. In most states, assault is committed only if the intended victim is aware of the impending battery. If you are physically struck but were not previously aware of the attacker's intention, then you cannot charge the attacker with committing assault because he has only committed battery. If you are soundly sleeping and a burglar strikes you with his weapon, he has only committed battery.

This means that if you as a martial arts student, misuse your techniques and commit a battery, you may well have also committed assault. If so, then you have committed two separate crimes, which makes you subject to two separate fines and/or jail sentences. Additionally, if you injure someone you may be subject to a civil lawsuit resulting in your having to pay damages to the injured person. (This is further discussed in detail in the section on civil court procedures.)

DISTURBING THE PEACE

This crime is referred to as breach of the peace in some states. Disorderly conduct is also another synonomous term. Basically, it consists of noisy and disturbing conduct. Included are loud and offensive arguing, profanity in public, fighting, or threatening to fight. Many states, however, consider fighting a separate crime. A few states classify fighting as a form of disturbing the peace. In all states, though, fighting and disturbing the peace are misdemeanors rather than felonies.

Thus if two persons become involved in a fight, and neither one charges the other with either assault or battery or files a civil lawsuit against the other person, an investigating police officer can charge them both with either fighting or disturbing the peace (assuming that self-defense from an attacker is not involved).

MALICIOUS MISCHIEF

Malicious mischief is a misdemeanor concerned with a person damaging the property of another. The law requires that there be actual physical damage done to the property. Deliberately knocking a bronze statue over, which upon being uprighted is seen to have suffered no damage, could not be malicious mischief.

Both real property and personal property are protected under the law. Real property includes real estate as well as anything attached to it. Examples of real property are fields, grass, flowers, gardens, trees, buildings, ponds, and streams. Personal property includes any personal item other than real property. Examples of personal property include cars, motorcycles, bicycles, clothes, furniture, appliances, and jewelry.

The law also requires deliberate and premeditated intent to cause physical damage to the property. As will be discussed in the topic of homicide, the intent to specifically cause physical damage is referred to as *malice*. The legal definition of malice concerns a person's state of mind and has nothing to do with hate or any other emotions toward the victim.

Following are some examples of malicious mischief. Note particularly those examples that involve the martial arts.

A group of people at a picnic in a public park go on a rampage and throw all the picnic tables, benches, and trash cans into the lake. They are guilty of committing malicious mischief even though the damage was done to public property.

In another example, several martial arts students are gathered on a street corner. They get into a discussion of the ability of each other's techniques. Bill accuses Ralph of having so weak and inaccurate a back kick that he doubted that Ralph could even kick the glass out of the nearby telephone booth door. Ralph, being intent on proving his ability, promptly back kicks every glass panel out of the lower half of the booth. Clearly having intent to cause physical damage to real property belonging to the phone company, Ralph is undeniably guilty of having committed malicious mischief.

George recently acquired a set of nunchakus and practices with them every day. One afternoon, several girls happen by as he is practicing. They make fun of him as he accidentally whacks himself in the back of the head. Being somewhat embarrassed but determined to improve his image, he sets a couple of bottles on a fence to break. During his demonstration, he also knocks out a few fence slats. This constitutes malicious mischief.

Two young men at a lounge are discussing the fact that one of them is a black belt. The other, not being a martial arts student, tries to put down the advantage the black belt might have in a fight because of his techniques. The black belt, unable to ignore the ridicule of his drinking mate, becomes a little upset. In the restroom together later in the evening, the black belt, in an attempt to impress his friend, punches and kicks several holes in the bathroom walls and kicks the soap dispenser off the wall. His intent to damage, together with his physical acts, constitute malicious damage.

MAYHEM OR MAIMING

Mayhem is a crime closely associated with battery. Mayhem is the crime of maiming your opponent. Maiming is the act of permanently crippling or disfiguring an opponent in a fight. The crime requires that the prosecution prove beyond a reasonable doubt that the maimer had definite intent to maim the victim. The proving of intent would, of course, imply that the crime was premeditated. In this context, premeditation may be preplanned several hours or just several minutes before the maiming occurs. However, if the maiming occurs spontaneously and unintentionally during a fight, then the lack of intent prevents prosecution for mayhem (although some other crime may be prosecuted for such as battery).

Various acts that are considered to maim include:

1. Cutting off or pulling off an ear.
2. Causing the loss of eyesight in one or both eyes.
3. Cutting out the tongue.
4. Disfiguring the nose by cutting or slitting it.
5. Severely cutting a lip.
6. Crippling a person's arm or leg permanently.
7. Intentionally knocking out a person's tooth.
8. Cutting off any part of the body.

In summary, then, maiming involves the cutting off or permanently crippling of any part of the body, provided such an injury is intentional, deliberate, and premeditated.

Since this crime can result in up to 20 years in prison or a sizeable fine, depending upon which state you are in, it is certainly worthwhile for any martial arts student to be aware of the crime. Although a very small minority of martial art students in the United States train with real bladed weapons, they should be aware of the potentially severe penalty should they misuse the weapon and disfigure an opponent in a defensive situation. By far, the majority of martial arts students in the United States train in styles employing no weapons other than the body itself. It is particularly for their benefit that the following example is offered.

Let us consider Howard who has trained for two years in a martial art. Fred has been seeing Howard's girl on the sly and Howard knows it. He waits outside Fred's store one night and meets him to settle the matter. For some time Howard has waited to "get even" with Fred and told some of his friends that he would "fix" Freddie boy but good. A fight starts and during the conflict, Howard deliberately kicks Fred's knee joint very hard from the side causing Fred to be permanently crippled in that leg. Without question, Howard is guilty of maiming Fred. (The issue of who struck the first blow in the fight is ignored in this example.)

HOMICIDE

Homicide is the killing of one human being by another human being. This is a topic of particular importance to martial arts students because of the seriousness of the crime if illegally committed. Additionally, as seen in Figure I–3, there are many aspects to the subject of homicide. All martial arts have techniques that are capable of resulting in the death of an opponent. Surely no one would argue with the moral precept that to needlessly and wantonly take a person's life is wrong. In the eyes of the law, there are only limited situations in which the taking of a life is warranted to the extent that the law will allow the homicide committer to go free without penalty of any sort. This, of course, is the situation of *self-defense*, which is discussed later in this section and elsewhere in the text.

Figure I–3 shows that there are two main categories of homicide—criminal and noncriminal, each of which is further divided. Noncriminal homicide is divided into excusable and justifiable homicides, the latter of which applies to self-defense situations. Criminal homicide is divided into murder and manslaughter. Manslaughter may be voluntary or involuntary. Murder is divided into first and second degree (and in some states into third degree). Second degree murder is further broken down into three categories—negligent homicide, felony murder, and homicide while resisting arrest. Let us now examine each of the categories of homicide.

CRIMINAL HOMICIDE

As seen in Figure I–3, criminal homicide has two primary divisions—murder and manslaughter.

Murder

Murder is any premeditated or intentional illegal killing of a person. Premeditation means that the killer thought about the

SCHEMATIC DIAGRAM OF THE CATEGORIES OF HOMICIDE

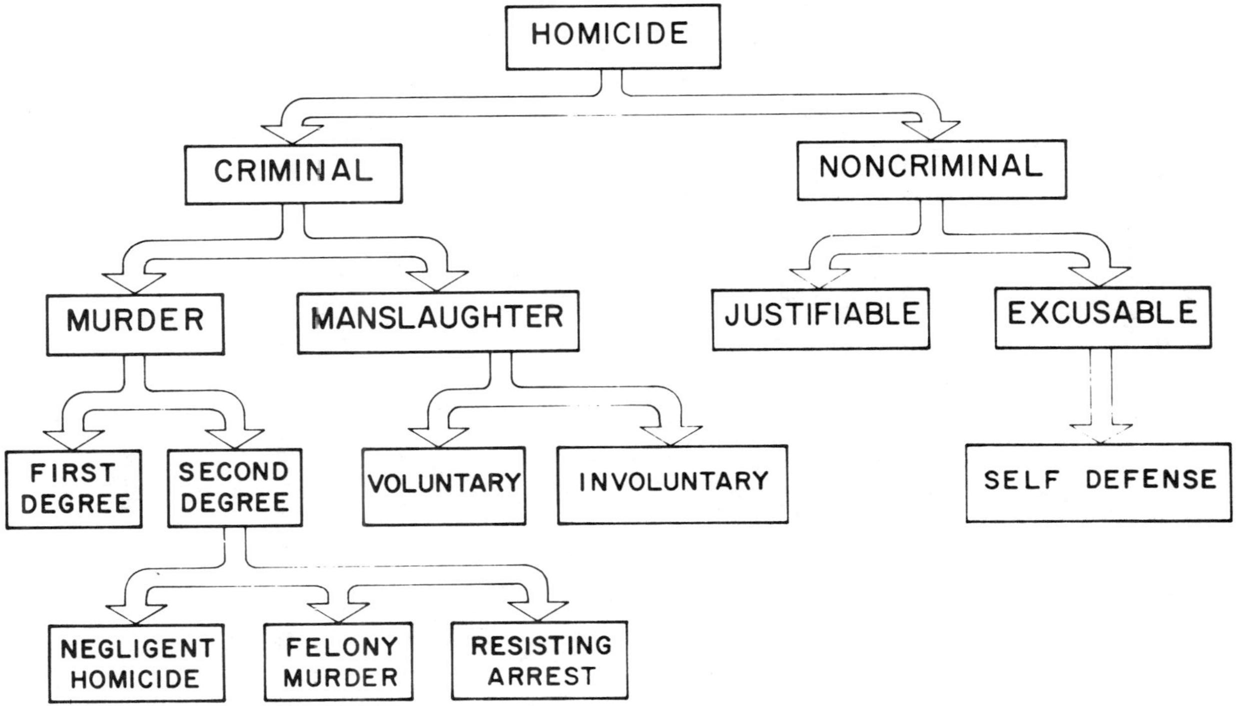

FIGURE I-3

homicide before he committed it, even if the thinking was only for a few seconds before the crime. This, of course, is the most serious type of homicide and, therefore, receives the most severe penalty under the law.

In the language of the legal profession, the premeditation indicates intent and is referred to as *malice* or *malice aforethought*. Thus our original definition of murder could be reworded to state that murder is the unlawful act of killing a person with malice aforethought. If the attacker's intent is only to commit serious bodily injury, but the victim's death results, then the attacker is considered to have committed murder because the death resulted from both the unlawful act and the intent (or malice). Malice, as used in the definition of murder, has nothing to do with disliking, hating, or having any ill feeling toward the victim. In fact, in many homicides, the attacker does not know the victim so there would be no feelings at all involved. Further, murder is homicide that lacks excuse or justification thereby distinguishing murder from noncriminal homicide.

First Degree

There are two kinds of malice—express and implied. It is the distinction between the two that provides the basis for separating first degree murder from second degree murder. Basically, first degree murder is the crime of killing with expressed malice. It may be said that expressed malice exists when an individual makes known, either through words or actions, the intent to kill another person. This type of malice is very clear, with the attacker leaving little or no doubt in anyone's mind as to intent.

Second Degree

Second degree murder is the crime of committing homicide with implied malice. Implied malice exists when an individual does not express any malice, but the presence of malice can be deduced. There are three main categories of second degree murder all of which originate from an attacker having no concern about the possible fatal results of his criminal actions, even though his intent is not to kill someone. Although this attacker does not preplan his homicide, he has such a disregard for human life in his actions that the law equates this with implied intent.

Figure I–3 shows that the three types of second degree murder include:

1. Negligent homicide.
2. Felony homicide.
3. Homicide while resisting arrest.

Negligent homicide. In the crime of negligent homicide, negligence refers to the utter and complete disregard of the safety and health of others, even though one has the knowledge that a specific act is highly dangerous. Negligence, in general, is the performance of an act that an average reasonable and prudent person would not commit. In the case of negligent homicide, the act is so dangerous that a death results. The unreasonableness of the killer in committing the act is assumed by the law to represent the intent required for the crime of murder.

Some examples will make the concept of negligent homicide clearer. Consider, for example, a man hiding behind a tall wooden fence. As some people walk by, he tosses a heavy piece of scrap metal over the fence to scare them. Instead, the metal hits one of the passersby on the head and kills him. In another example, a man hides in the woods alongside a highway. As trucks go by, he takes "potshots" with his small calibre rifle to frighten the truck drivers. In the process, a bullet strikes a passenger in the head, killing him. In a third example, a young man throws rocks at a passing train to scare the passengers when the rocks loudly bang against the metal side of the car. One of the rocks breaks a passenger car window and kills a passenger. In each of these examples, the death results from a person performing a highly dangerous act having a strong likelihood of resulting in serious injury or death. Yet the performer has complete disregard and lack of concern for the probable consequences of what he is doing. The law would thus say he is just as guilty of having committed murder as if he had started with complete intent to kill someone.

Felony murder. The second category of second degree murder is felony murder. This is a criminal homicide that occurs during the act of committing a felony. Even if the homicide is an accident, if it occurs during the commission of a felony, it is considered felony murder. The accidental death would be, in effect, a negligent homicide but would not be called that in this instance.

The felonies that felony murder can be charged in are the more serious crimes such as armed robbery, arson, rape, and murder, etc. During the commission of any of these felonies, it may not be the intent of the felon to commit homicide. However, if anyone should be killed during the crime, then the court will not accept the excuse that the killing was accidental or unintended. The law interprets that the commission of a felony is a highly dangerous act inherent with the risk that a death could result. For anyone to act in such an unreasonable and imprudent manner is considered to indicate the presence of malice or intent.

The felony murder doctrine, or rule, holds all felons responsible for the death of anyone occurring during commission of the felony regardless of who does the actual killing. This includes the death of a fellow felon, a police officer (even if accidentally killed by other police officers), or any innocent bystanders or third parties. Some examples will make the discussion clearer. For example, if an arsonist, in burning a building, kills one or more occupants, then he is guilty of felony murder. If a bank robber deliberately kills a police officer, he has committed a felony murder. If a bank robber kills an innocent bystander while attempting to escape, this too is felony murder. Suppose several men are robbing a bank and one accidentally kills one of his partners when his trigger finger slips. Each of the surviving felons are guilty of felony murder regardless of which one actually did the shooting. A man who strangles a woman while committing rape is guilty of felony murder. Consider the man who schemes to murder his business partner by poisoning his liquor. When both the partner and his wife die from the poison, then the schemer has committed both murder (the partner) and felony murder (the wife).

In each of the previous examples, the law would hold all of the participating felons guilty of felony murder. Even in the examples where unintentional deaths accidentally occurred, the law would interpret the dangerous acts as being so irresponsible as to indicate intent to kill.

Resisting arrest. The third category of second degree murder, as shown in Figure I–3, is homicide committed while resisting arrest. The law includes within this crime not only a police officer killed intentionally or unintentionally while making an arrest, but also any bystander who might be killed accidentally during the arrest attempt. The degree of force used in the resisting attempt is irrelevant. It is the event of death, regardless of how it occurred, that constitutes the crime.

For example, the suspect may only wish to delay the arresting officer for some reason. During the minor physical skirmish that occurs, the police officer trips and hits his head on the sidewalk resulting in his death. Even though the suspect intended no injury whatsoever to the officer, some states would nevertheless hold the suspect guilty of second degree murder. A stronger example is where the suspect vigorously resists arrest and uses a weapon (such as a club, gun, or knife) to aid his resistance. Should he thereby kill the officer, then most states would hold him guilty of second degree murder. This would not be first degree murder because it is assumed in the example that the suspect had not earlier plotted to kill the officer. The death occurred on the spot due to the circumstances of the instant and therefore is not premeditated.

Manslaughter

Now that we have discussed the various aspects of murder,

let us examine the second category of criminal homicide—manslaughter, which is separated into voluntary and involuntary manslaughter. The basic difference between murder and manslaughter is that whereas murder is premeditated, manslaughter is not. In other words it can be said that murder is homicide with malice aforethought; whereas, manslaughter is homicide without malice aforethought.

Voluntary Manslaughter

The crime of voluntary manslaughter occurs when a person commits a homicide while under the influence of excessively strong emotions. Manslaughter often is the result of intense provocation causing a person to lose control of what would otherwise be reasonable and prudent judgment. Since manslaughter occurs as a result of the circumstances and is not preplanned, as is murder, the law imposes a less severe punishment for manslaughter than for murder. That is to say, the law is more sympathetic toward someone who commits a homicide while in a blind rage than toward a person who schemes ahead of time to commit a homicide.

In order for a homicide to be ruled as manslaughter rather than murder, it must be demonstrated that:

1. A legally recognized provocation existed to prompt the slayer's act of killing.
2. The provocation drove the attacker into a fit of rage or extreme passion.
3. The attacker killed the victim while in this mental state.

Some of the provocations recognized by the law as justification for voluntary manslaughter include:

1. Assault.
2. Battery.
3. Sexual attack and adultery.

4. Insults.
5. Trespass.
6. Resisting illegal arrest.
7. Inoperative self-defense.

Assault. As previously discussed, assault is an apparent attempt to commit bodily injury against a person sufficient to create fear in that person's mind. Simple assault in all courts would probably never be sufficient reason for committing homicide, however. The law places a value on human life such that a threat to punch you in the nose does not justify your killing the threatening attacker.

On the other hand, assault with a deadly weapon (such as a gun, club, or knife) does constitute sufficient provocation in some states to reduce a murder charge to voluntary manslaughter. In such an instance, the court would apply the test of what a reasonable man would have believed of the attacker in the same situation. The victim's assault must have been credible enough to have provoked the slayer into believing he was truly in danger of being injured and also to have created a blind fear in the slayer's mind sufficient to cloud his reason. This is not a case of self-defense because assault is merely an apparent attempt against a person.

What this means to martial arts students is that an apparent attempt to physically injure a person does not warrant taking the assaulter's life. If you do kill the assaulter, you may be charged with murder. Your attorney, at best, can get the criminal charge reduced to voluntary manslaughter. If the assault, even with a deadly weapon, appears to be leading to an apparent dangerous situation, a temporary disabling of the opponent would be justified, but homicide would not be acceptable nor necessary.

Battery against you. Battery, as earlier detailed, is the making of unlawful physical contact against a person. The law has determined that if the battery is performed with sufficient force and intensity against a person and throws the victim into a blind rage, it could be sufficient provocation to result in voluntary manslaughter. A slap in the face, a punch in the nose, or a kick in the shins would not constitute sufficient provocations for committing homicide. The attack must be forceful enough to cause pain and bloodshed to warrant classifying a resulting homicide as manslaughter versus murder.

The significance here for the martial arts student is that only if your attacker is beating you with the obvious intent of doing great bodily harm are you justified in killing him. Even in these circumstances, in some states, you may not be justified in killing the attacker unless there is virtually no alternative in order to save yourself. There is a close distinction here between the concept of self-defense and voluntary manslaughter. This point will be discussed in detail in the section on self-defense. However, it is most important that you realize that when defending yourself, if you kill your attacker after he strikes you, you may possibly be charged with voluntary manslaughter.

Battery against a relative. It is generally considered sufficient provocation to classify a homicide as voluntary manslaughter which results from the slayer witnessing the victim committing severe battery against a relative. As with battery against you, battery against a relative is not a legal provocation sufficient to reduce murder to manslaughter unless the battery was of strong force and intensity.

Battery against a nonrelative. At present, the law in most states would not allow the killing of an attacker of a close friend or any third party to constitute provocation to reduce murder to manslaughter. As discussed in the self-defense section, you may go to the aid of a third party being attacked but homicide is very rarely allowed under the law in such a case.

Sexual attack and adultery. For sexual crimes (rape, seduction) or adultery to constitute sufficient provocation to reduce murder to voluntary manslaughter, the killing must occur immediately after the slayer discovers the act in progress. The discovery of the act must create a severe fit of passion or rage in the slayer's mind sufficient to affect his self-control and ability to reason. He must commit the homicide while in this state of mind, thus the requirement of immediacy for the homicide. With the passage of time, perhaps just a few minutes, the normal state of mind will return. If the homicide is committed after the rage passes, then the charge would be murder rather than manslaughter.

As an example, Henry comes home and finds his wife engaged in sexual intercourse with the milkman. Henry flies into a wild rage and immediately kills the milkman. The court would find Henry guilty of committing voluntary manslaughter. (If he also killed his wife while enraged, that would be murder.) Suppose, on the other hand, that Henry goes into a rage and yells at the milkman to get out. Four days later Henry attacks and kills the milkman. He would be charged with murder as the court would interpret that four days was sufficient time for Henry to cool down and regain his normal self-control and power of reasoning. As a different example, suppose Henry comes home and finds the milkman raping his daughter. In a fit of rage, he kills the milkman. This, again, would be voluntary manslaughter as long as the homicide was committed while in an uncontrolled state of mind.

Insults. It is a general rule of law that insults, abusive language, or words of any nature, unaccompanied by battery, do not constitute sufficient provocation to reduce a charge of murder to a lesser charge of voluntary manslaughter. There are a very few courts, however, which believe that there are limited situations in which certain abusive language might be considered provocation.

It is advised, however, that any martial arts student should not take defensive physical action against a person based merely on what that person says. This advice should be followed regardless of what someone says to you. There probably will be (and have been) times when you very much want to strike someone for a nasty remark to you or someone with you. Keep in mind that if your strike leads to a fight and the person is killed by you, you can be charged with murder but probably not voluntary manslaughter.

Trespass. Trespass, in this sense, means to pass onto a person's property without permission. Trespass upon one's property is sufficient provocation to reduce a charge of murder to manslaughter only if the trespass is accompanied by some additional aggravating and dangerous felony act by the trespasser. Examples of additional aggravations include assault and battery and destruction of property. The law does not consider nonfelonious trespass sufficient justification to take the life of an individual.

As an example, suppose a man is taking a shortcut through your large field but is merely walking causing no damage. Although you are legally justified in evicting a trespasser from your property, you may not kill him for simple trespass. In fact, you may not use force to evict him unless he actively resists being evicted. As a different example, assume the man is not only trespassing on your field but also is setting your house on fire. Should you become enraged to the point that you lose your sense of reason and in the ensuing fight kill him, you will have committed voluntary manslaughter and not murder.

Resisting illegal arrest. Some states allow homicide committed while resisting illegal or unlawful arrest to constitute sufficient provocation to classify the killing as voluntary manslaughter. Most states, however, would consider the killing of a police officer while attempting to arrest a suspect, illegally or legally, as murder. Those states designating the crime voluntary manslaughter would consider such provocations as:

1. Attempted arrest using an incorrect warrant (wrong or misspelled name, wrong address).
2. Refusal of officer to identify himself as a police officer.
3. The officer attempts to make the arrest outside of his area of legal jurisdiction.

Since the objective of this book is to describe the law in general, no attempt has been made to determine in which states this class of homicide is manslaughter versus murder. The significance to the martial arts student is that no attempt to arrest you should be resisted even if you are certain that the arrest is unlawful. Should you be arrested, for any reason whether legitimate or not, you should immediately seek the assistance of a lawyer—whether you hire one or have the court appoint one on your behalf. As will be discussed in the sections on criminal and civil court procedures, there are ample safeguards to your rights such that any legal errors made in arresting you will be quickly detected by an attorney. The prearrest and arrest procedures are not 100% fail-safe. Occasionally an unfortunate error may result in the arrest of the wrong person. Should that happen to you, submit peacefully to the arrest. In no instance would an illegal arrest in the United States justify the killing or the injuring of the arresting officer.

Inoperative self-defense. Inoperative self-defense refers to a situation where a homicide occurred which normally would be considered self-defense except for a factor existing which cancels the excuse of self-defense.

For example, consider a situation in which a person is receiving a severe beating from an opponent. In order to save himself, and having no other alternative, he kills the opponent. The doctrine of self-defense (discussed in detail later) would normally excuse the slayer in such a situation. However, if the slayer initiated the attack by delivering the first strike, then he cannot be excused. Provided the severe counterattack against him drove him into a state of uncontrolled rage, he would be guilty of voluntary manslaughter.

This is an important point for martial arts students. If you deliver the first strike in a fight without sufficient reason prompting you and you kill the other person during the ensuing fight (which you started), you will have committed voluntary manslaughter. (If your first strike kills the other person and you were not justified in so doing, you will have committed murder.)

A second example is due to a mistake of fact on the part of the slayer. Suppose you, as a martial arts student, find yourself in a situation where you sincerely believe that it is necessary to kill your attacker in order to save yourself. Subsequent to your opponent's death, it turns out that your assessment of the facts was wrong and it was not necessary to kill the other person. In most jurisdictions you have committed voluntary manslaughter.

As a third example, assume that you go beyond the reasonable amount of force necessary to disable an attacker thereby resulting in his death. Perhaps a young man without any weapons tries to beat you with his fists in a parking lot and you knock him down and then kill him after he is disabled and down. This would be an unreasonable defense making you guilty of manslaughter.

Involuntary Manslaughter

It can be stated that involuntary manslaughter is an unintended (without malice aforethought) homicide committed while engaged in an unlawful act less serious than a felony. Figure I–3 shows that this is the second category of manslaughter under criminal homicides. Involuntary manslaughter differs from voluntary manslaughter in that involuntary manslaughter means homicide without intention whereas voluntary manslaughter means intentional homicide. Manslaughter, in general, is not premeditated; whereas, murder is premeditated. The following examples will illustrate the nature of involuntary manslaughter.

For example, a man steals $15 from a lady in the park. As he is attempting to escape on a motorcycle, he accidentally kills a pedestrian. Since the $15 theft was not a felony, then the homicide is considered involuntary manslaughter rather than felony murder.

As a second example, a doctor performs an illegal operation and the patient dies. This is involuntary manslaughter because the death was not intentional and the unlawful act was not a felony. In some jurisdictions, an abortion would be an illegal operation.

A third example concerns gross negligence resulting in an unintentional homicide. Of interest to the martial arts student is the student who lives in a state allowing possession of nunchakus. The student, in an attempt to impress his friends at work, begins wildly swinging the nunchakus, laughing, and attempting to frighten everyone watching. In his reckless eagerness, he strikes an onlooker in the head and kills him. In some states, the reckless and negligent misuse of a deadly weapon is considered involuntary manslaughter. For the purpose of the martial arts, you can construct different examples by taking the previous example and simply inserting different weapons. The student attempts to show off his ability with the sai, a kung-fu sword, throwing a shuriken, a tonfa, a wooden fighting staff, etc. and kills an onlooker. In each instance, the negligent and careless use of the weapon constitutes involuntary manslaughter.

NONCRIMINAL HOMICIDE

Noncriminal homicide contains all those homicides which the law will not prosecute because it places no guilt on the person committing the homicide. Figure I–3 shows that there are two categories of noncriminal homicide—excusable and justifiable. The primary difference between the two is that, although excusable homicides are normally illegal acts, the law excuses their commission; whereas, justifiable homicides are not illegal acts. Let us now examine each of the two categories in greater detail.

Justifiable Homicide

There are certain homicides in the United States that are considered legal to commit. In fact, the government or the courts may actually order that certain homicides be committed thereby relieving the slayer of any legal liability or responsibility for the resulting death. The following are examples of justifiable homicide:

1. The court ordered execution of a felon.
2. The killing by law officers or soldiers of citizens involved in a riot, armed uprising, or rebellion.
3. The killing of enemy troops by a member of the armed forces during a state of war.
4. The killing of a felon by a police officer during an at-

tempted arrest or an attempt to prevent escape.

5. The committing of a homicide in the name of self-defense in order to stop a felon from causing severe physical injury during the commission of a felony.

Excusable Homicide

Excusable homicides are those killings that the law would normally consider illegal; however, under the particular circumstances of these cases, the homicides are excused. That is to say, the slayer is freed from any legal responsibility or liability for the death. This is the homicide category under which most deaths resulting from legal self-defense acts will fall. This category also includes accidental deaths resulting from non-negligent causes. (Remember that accidental deaths resulting from negligent causes are considered involuntary manslaughter.)

There are two main types of excusable homicides:

1. Homicide due to accident.
2. Homicide due to self-defense.

An example of an accidental homicide would be the case of a man mowing his yard and the mower throws out a rock killing a small child standing nearby. The death was obviously unintentional and could not be attributed to the negligence of the adult. It was simply an unfortunate accident and the homicide is therefore excused by the law.

The topic of self-defense will be discussed in a separate section of the text.

Chapter 4

DOCTRINE OF SELF-DEFENSE

The legal doctrine of self-defense may be stated as follows:

> Any person fearing death or serious bodily harm from the assault and/or battery of an attacker has the legal right to defend himself using a reasonable amount of force, but may kill the attacker only if necessary to save his own life.

It is a time honored principle that one is entitled to defend himself from physical attack by another person. Unfortunately, the law, being as complex as it is today, will not allow the issue to remain that simple. As the discussion proceeds, the reader will see that there are a number of aspects to consider in the name of self-defense.

First consider the point at which the law allows self-defensive action to begin. As explained in the section on assault, mere words uttered by a person, regardless of how abusive, vile, insulting, or threatening, are not sufficient grounds for using physical force in the name of self-defense. If the person, in addition to verbally threatening a physical attack, openly acts such that any reasonable person would anticipate, or fear, that the attacker was going to cause bodily injury, then self-defense would be justified. More simply stated, you do not have to be physically struck or injured before self-defense is legally justifiable. Nor does your attacker have to be in the process of actively physically attacking you before self-defense is legally justifiable. If your attacker has both threatened you verbally and acts such that you honestly believe he is going to attempt to injure you, then self-defense, using a reasonable amount of force for the situation is generally justifiable.

Consider the following examples to illustrate the preceding discussion. Suppose that I strike you with a baseball bat and you, in turn, knock me unconscious with a punch. There is no doubt that you have justifiably and legally defended yourself. As a second example, suppose that I call you various foul names and threaten to hit you with my baseball bat which is at home in my closet. You may not legally or justifiably use physical force against me in the name of self-defense because you are in no danger of bodily injury by my mere verbal abuse. The bat is located someplace else, and I obviously am no physical threat to you with it. In the third example, suppose that I swear at you and swing a wild punch but miss striking you. Legally, you may use a reasonable amount of force against me in order to defend yourself because I am obviously attempting to physically injure you. It is immaterial that I have not yet actually touched you. This simply means that, at this point, I have committed assault but not yet battery. As a last example, assume that I threaten to cut you with my knife and reach into my jacket pocket as I take a step forward. Although you cannot yet determine whether or not I actually have a knife in my pocket, legally you may act to defend youself. My actions in this example are such as to convince any reasonable person that I have a knife in my possession with which I intend to commit bodily injury.

A further point to consider is your right to self-defense in the event that your attacker, who has beaten you, suddenly stops and walks away. The previous discussion established that you may legally defend yourself while the beating is in progress or when the attacker acts such that he obviously intends to beat you. But here we are talking about the attack having clearly ceased and the attacker is obviously leaving. At this point, then, you are no longer in danger of being physically injured. Under the law, you may not now pursue your attacker and strike him. Nor may you throw any object at him and thereby injure him.

This well-established principle is based on the interpretation that after the attacker has ceased his attack and is leaving, a time lapse occurs during which self-defense is no longer warranted. Instead, any physical attack subsequently delivered by the victim against the departing attacker will be considered retaliation and not self-defense. This twist of the law would thus make the original victim liable for battery upon the attacker if the victim retaliated. The complexity of the law thus burdens the victim of an attack with suitable timing for his defensive actions. A delay in initiating his defense may subject him to criminal charges or civil lawsuit. Of course, in this discussion it should be kept in mind that the original attacker is guilty of having committed battery upon the original victim.

Although this particular aspect of law (concerning retaliation) may seem initially unreasonable, further reflection reveals that it is probably quite fair. For example, how much time should be granted to an attacker in his departure before you would be willing not to strike him after he hit you? An answer by the lawyers would require a standard definition for the law books. How about twenty seconds? Two minutes? It would seem that a time definition is not adequate. How about a distance definition then? How far would it be reasonable to allow the attacker to go before striking him would no longer be self-defense? Ten feet? Two city blocks? It would seem that the law has already provided the best answer. Once your attacker ceases using physical force and is departing, the rule of self-defense no longer applies. Your recourse at this point is through the law, not through physical force. Your attacker may be liable for either civil or criminal assault and battery.

Let us digress for a moment to a previous example. The attacker threatened to cut you with his knife and as he took a step toward you, reached into his jacket pocket. You, as a reasonable and prudent person, interpret his actions as an intended physical attack. Being aware of your legal right to self-defense, you strike him very hard in the midsection thereby knocking his breath out and bruising his ribs. If he really has a knife in his pocket which he honestly intended to cut you with, you clearly acted justifiably. But what if he has no knife and was playing a practical joke on you in order to laugh at your frightened reaction? How does the law classify your actions? Are you now guilty of having committed battery on your pseudo-attacker?

According to the law, you acted justifiably if any reasonable person in similar circumstances also would have interpreted the attacker's actions as indicating bodily injury was imminent. Stated otherwise, your opponent's bluff or acting was realistic enough such that you, or anyone else of sound mind, would have believed that he indeed did possess a knife. If your attacker sues you for civil damages, however, and you find yourself at a jury trial, it will be the jury's duty to determine the reasonableness of your belief in the supposed imminent attack. (It is a jury's duty to determine the facts in a trial.) It is not necessary that an actual danger of your bodily injury existed. Even though you were mistaken about the existence of your attacker's knife, it was a reasonable interpretation, based on your opponent's words and actions, that a knife did exist which would be used against you.

As another example, consider a person approaching you and pointing a pistol at your head. You, as a well-trained student of the martial arts, defend yourself but seriously injure your would-be attacker. If the gun was loaded and his intentions actually were to shoot you, then your defense was legally justifiable. However, what if the gun were not loaded and only a joke was intended? Again, the apparent danger is what you responded to. You would be justified in acting as you did if any other reasonable and prudent person would have interpreted the situation as you did.

Referring back to the doctrine of self-defense as earlier defined, it is seen that this provides a legal excuse for the commission of homicide under certain conditions. However, it cannot be stressed strongly enough that you should kill your attacker only if there is absolutely no other choice and your life is in imminent danger. "No other choice" means that you have no possibility of retreat from your attacker. (The issue of retreat will be discussed in more detail shortly.) The lack of choice further means that any use of force other than killing your opponent will continue to place your life in imminent danger.

In effect, this issue means that this is a situation which you, as a defender, might interpret as excusable homicide under the doctrine of self-defense. To reiterate, before you take the life of an attacker, be absolutely certain that there is no other choice in order to save your own life. Remember that a prosecutor may argue that you, as a practitioner of a martial art, should have sufficient knowledge and control to be able to stop any attacker without the necessity of taking his life. This is probably a valid argument, particularly if you have trained for some period of time. Assume that you hold an advanced rank and have killed someone in self-defense. How would you answer the prosecutor's argument?

The jury will judge your actions under the standard of reasonableness. They will determine how a reasonable and prudent person would have acted under similar circumstances in order to determine whether or not the homicide was a necessity.

A further factor that will be examined is that of the presence or absence of fear in the defendant (the one who committed the homicide). The doctrine of self-defense as earlier defined began "Any person fearing . . .". It is most important that fear is truly present when defending oneself, especially if the attacker is killed by the defender. The jury, in such a case, will apply the standard of reasonableness. That is, it will be determined if a reasonable person in similar circumstances would be truly fearful of death or serious bodily harm. Additionally, it will have to be clearly evident to the jury that the defendant actually was fearful during his defensive actions. The lack of fear on the part of the defendant may be interpreted as intent should the attacker be killed, resulting in a charge of manslaughter rather than acquittal for self-defense. If you have no fear of your attacker's ability to do you serious bodily harm due to confidence in your martial art techniques, you should definitely avoid killing your attacker. To kill an attacker when you feel in control of the situation will be unwarranted and needless in the eyes of the court. The result may well be the finding of manslaughter against you. Even worse, if it is proven that you deliberately killed your opponent in self-defense, then the charge may be murder.

When attacked, should you retreat? There is not yet unanimous opinion among the states on this issue. Although this remains a controversial issue, the majority view is expressed as the Texas rule. This rule states:

> An individual, who is not a trespasser, need not retreat from an assailant if he (the defender) truly fears death or serious bodily harm.

It is assumed under this rule that the assailant is the person who initiated the attack without any provocation on the part of the defender. Some of the states following this majority view include Texas, Oklahoma, Oregon, Arizona, Colorado, West Virginia, Kansas, and Kentucky.

A second view on the issue of retreat from an attacker is that a defender, who is not a trespasser, need not retreat from an assailant to defend himself if the assailant is attempting to commit a felony against the defender. In any other situation, the defender must retreat. Some of the states following this second viewpoint include North Carolina, Ohio, Washington, and Alabama.

A third view, representing the minority viewpoint, on the issue of retreat, states that a defender must always retreat from an assailant if such retreat is possible and safe. The only exception provided for under these jurisdictions is when the defender is being attacked within his own home. Only in your home, under this viewpoint, may you stand your ground to defend yourself. Some of the states following this minority viewpoint include Connecticut, New York, Iowa, and Michigan.

The conflicting viewpoints of various states on the issue of retreat in self-defense creates a dilemma for martial arts students. First, of course, it is necessary to know the law of the state in which you live should you have to defend yourself. To be certain of the law, you may have to get the advice of an attorney.

The second dilemma is the problem created by instructors

who teach their students never to retreat in a fight. Such an admonition is a carryover from centuries past when honor in battle was all important. "Saving face" in the Orient is most important even today. Thus it is likely that Oriental and Oriental-indoctrinated instructors will pass this tenet on to their students. Sometimes this retreating from an attacker might be interpreted as an act of cowardice. Although these are all different views of retreating from an attacker, they have no bearing on the legal status of retreat in each state. Regardless of whether one argues the moral viewpoint, the historical viewpoint, the militaristic viewpoint, the sociological viewpoint, the face-saving viewpoint, etc., it is indeed the viewpoint of the courts, backed by the law statutes, that determines whether or not an individual must retreat or not when attacked. Violation of these statutes is punishable by the courts; therefore, in order for you to avoid criminal charges or civil lawsuit arising out of your ignorance of the law, it will be worthwhile to determine the exact status of your state's viewpoint on the issue of retreat.

The majority viewpoint of states concerning the defense of others is that a person may defend blood relatives, marriage relatives, and total strangers from an attacker. Unfortunately, a dilemma is again posed for the martial arts student. Suppose you arrive on the scene after the attack has begun. How will you determine which party began the attack? There may be more to the situation than is readily obvious to you. Without doubt, the killing of an attacker in order to save a third person (relative or stranger) is very risky unless you know the entire situation and there is virtually no other way to save the third person. As mentioned elsewhere in this text, the court will determine both the reasonableness and the necessity of such a killing. There is always the possibility of an argument being made by the prosecutor that a martial arts student who has trained for some time should have enough control of his techniques to be able to control an attacker without killing him. The safest and most prudent course of action is to resort to the killing of an attacker only when all else fails and there is no other choice possible. If the court determines that even a single other choice was available to you, and yet you killed the attacker, then a charge of manslaughter or murder may be brought against you.

The minority view is that a person defending a stranger commits excusable homicide if he kills the attacker due to his (the defender's) interpretation of the situation. Additionally, it must be determined that the defender acted as would any person of ordinary prudence and reason. In fact, excusable homicide will be ruled in these jurisdictions even if the defender backed the wrong party (that is, he backed the attacker by mistake rather than the victim). It is only necessary that the defender prove that his interpretation of the fight scene was such that any other person would have made the same interpretation.

Generally, the commission of homicide while protecting property, either possessions or land, is neither justifiable nor excusable under the law. One exception to this general rule is the circumstance in which a person commits homicide while defending his home. However, this exception does not allow the killing of a mere trespasser on one's property.

Finally, it is necessary to point out the widespread misconception that martial arts students, and particularly black belts, may not use their techniques to defend themselves. This misconception is entirely incorrect with no legal validity. Under the laws of the United States, every citizen has the right to defend himself against unjustified physical attack. This defensive right allows the use of a "reasonable amount of force" for the situation. There is no law against using martial arts techniques for self-defense. However, misuse of martial arts techniques could be considered as assault or battery with a deadly weapon (the deadly weapon being the hand or foot), a more serious crime than simple assault or battery. Additionally there is no law in any state requiring martial arts students or instructors of any rank to register their hands with the police.

Part II

CRIMINAL LAW PROCEDURE

Introduction

CRIMINAL PROCEDURE

In the first part of the book, the various crimes were described in which one might be involved when using or misusing the techniques of the martial arts. The discussion was wide-ranging in order to give the reader as broad a base in crimes as possible. Part II of the book will be concerned with criminal procedure. This procedure encompasses all the police and criminal court procedures that occur, or might occur, should one be arrested and possibly consequently charged with committing a crime.

The section begins with a description of the court systems in the United States. Following this is a discussion of police procedures followed in making an arrest of a person suspected of committed a crime. The discussion then proceeds logically to court procedures which follow arrest. Included are pre-trial procedures, the trial itself, and possible post-trial conviction procedures.

Overall, this part of the book is designed to make the reader aware of what to expect should he be arrested on suspicion of having committed a crime. Although intended for use by students of the martial arts, the description of criminal court procedures would apply to the commission of any crime regardless of whether or not self-defense or any martial arts were involved.

It is hoped that the reader develops a sense that, although the American criminal legal system is complex, it is logical in its operation; and, most importantly, its processes are designed to protect the rights of the suspect at all times, even if found guilty. Because of the complexity of criminal law procedures, it should be obvious that if a person is charged with a crime, an attorney should be obtained at the earliest possible moment. The sooner you obtain legal professional help, the sooner that you may be assured that your Constitutional and statutory rights are being protected.

Part II deals only with criminal procedures; whereas, Part III will be concerned only with civil court procedures.

Chapter 5

THE CRIMINAL COURT SYSTEM

STATE COURTS

Within each state there are various levels of courts designed to deal with the various levels of seriousness of crimes. As earlier discussed, the level of seriousness may range from violation of a minor local ordinance (such as a parking violation) to commission of a serious felony (such as first degree murder). Figure II–1 illustrates the generalized scheme of a state court system. It should be noted, however, that not all state court systems will fit this scheme. As this book is generalized for all states, specific states may vary from the generalized discussion.

LOCAL COURTS

At the lowest level within the state court system is the justice of the peace court. This is a local court found in small rural areas. Its criminal jurisdiction is primarily limited to handling traffic violations, although some states allow jurisdiction over misdemeanors also. All justices of the peace have authority to hold a criminal suspect, brought before them by a law enforcement officer, for trial in a higher court if the justice thinks there is sufficient evidence present in the case.

Thus if you reside in or visit a small rural town and are suspected of having committed a misdemeanor, in some states you will be brought before a justice of the peace subsequent to arrest. In other states the justice of the peace can order you held in jail for hearing before a higher court having the jurisdiction to try the misdemeanor. In all states, the justice of the peace court cannot try a felony suspect, but it can order the suspect held for a hearing in a higher trial court having jurisdiction over felony offenses.

COUNTY AND MUNICIPAL COURTS

The next state courts to consider are the county and municipal criminal courts. As shown in Figure II–1, this layer of courts primarily handles misdemeanor criminal charges and usually not felony charges. The name of this layer of courts varies from state to state, being called county court in some states or municipal courts in other states. These courts also have authority to hold felony suspects for hearing in a higher trial court under whose jurisdiction trial of the suspect lies.

If you live in a larger town or city and commit, or are suspected at having committed, a misdemeanor, you may expect to be brought into a county or municipal court for hearing and trial. Further, if you are suspected of having committed a felony, you may be brought before a municipal or county judge and ordered held in jail in order to appear at a later time before a court having jurisdiction over felonies.

Juvenile offenses are handled by the juvenile court which exists as a separate court from the adult criminal courts. Figure I–1 shows the maximum ages at which juvenile courts have jurisdiction over youths.

STATE FELONY COURTS

At the next higher level of seriousness of crimes (as shown in Figure II–1) are the state felony courts. These courts actually

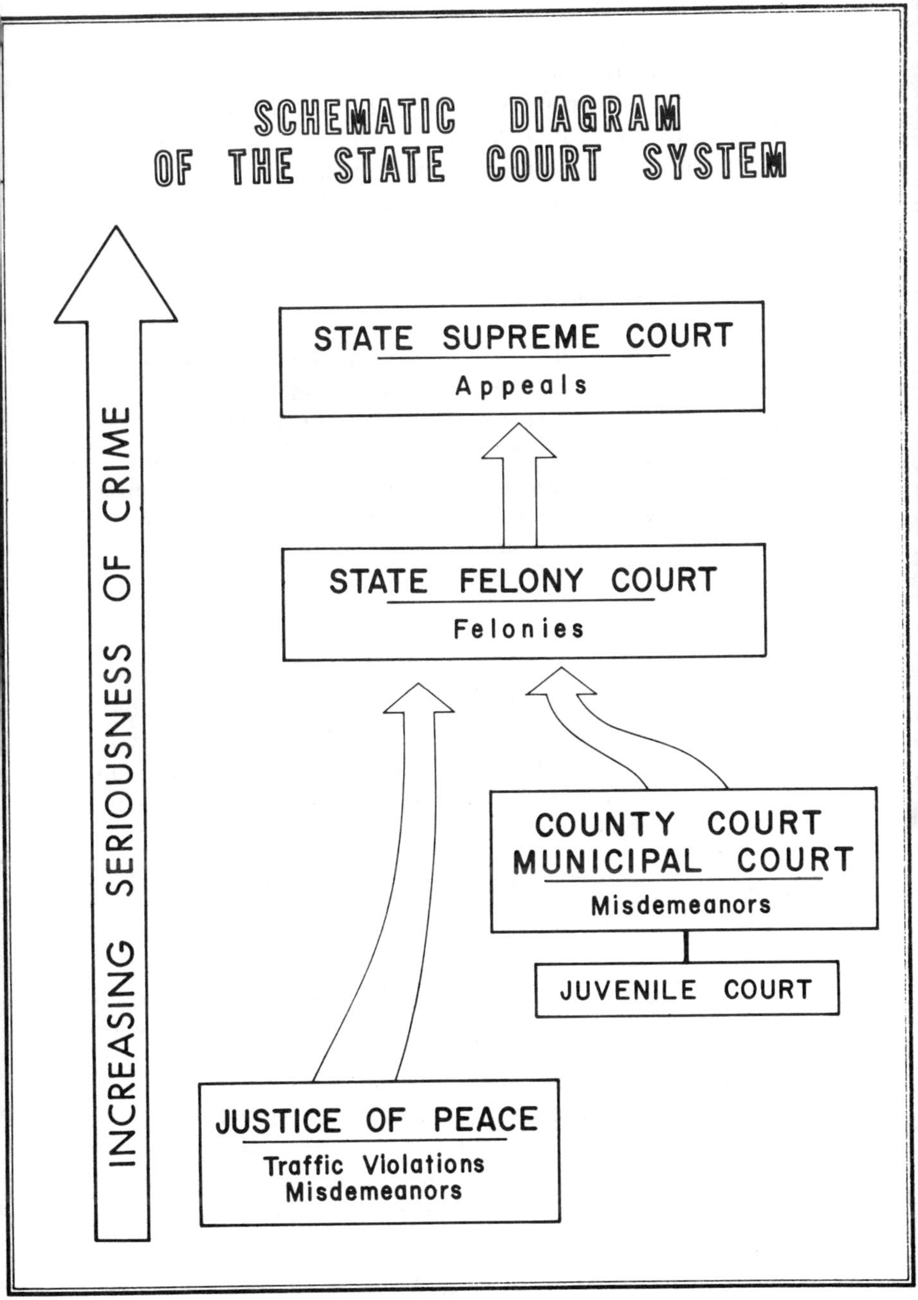
SCHEMATIC DIAGRAM
OF THE STATE COURT SYSTEM
INCREASING SERIOUSNESS OF CRIME
STATE SUPREME COURT
Appeals
STATE FELONY COURT
Felonies
COUNTY COURT
MUNICIPAL COURT
Misdemeanors
JUVENILE COURT
JUSTICE OF PEACE
Traffic Violations
Misdemeanors

FIGURE II–1

serve two purposes in the court system. First, they are the trial courts primarily concerned with trying felony cases. Second, they act as courts of appeal for the lower levels of courts (justice of the peace, county, and municipal) previously discussed.

Due to the variation in state court systems, this level of state courts is designated by differing names in various states. They are variously called the circuit court or the superior court. The state of New York confused the issue by naming this level of court the "supreme court."

In most states, then, if you are suspected of having committed a felony, you may expect to be brought into a circuit or superior court for hearing and trial. Additionally, if you have been convicted of a lesser crime, such as a misdemeanor, in a lower level court (justice of the peace, county, or municipal) and wish to appeal the decision, your attorney will most probably bring the appeal to a circuit or superior court.

STATE SUPREME COURTS

The final and highest level of state courts is the state supreme court level (see Figure II–I). In legal terminology, this is "the court of last resort," which means that there is no higher level of state judicial authority. This court is basically a court of appeal to which lower court decision may be appealed for review. It is not a court of original criminal jurisdiction because misdemeanor and felony charges would not originally be brought by this court; rather, the charges would originate in a lower level of court.

Consequently, if you are convicted of a felony or misdemeanor in a lower court and have exhausted your appeal efforts to other state courts, the highest and last state court to which you may appeal for reversal of your conviction is the state supreme court. (In New York state it is the Court of Appeals since New York's "supreme court" is actually a lower level court.)

Failing to win a favorable appeal decision in the state supreme court, a convicted criminal may appeal no higher, with one exception. If the case involves a question of constitutionality under the United States Constitution, then an appeal may be made to the United States Supreme Court. This special procedure is discussed later.

FEDERAL COURTS

The second system of courts that exists in the United States, in addition to the system of state courts just discussed, is the federal court system. As shown in Figure II–2, there are three levels of federal criminal courts. Although there are other federal courts in the federal system, they are not part of the criminal court system and therefore are not discussed here. Authority for existence of this court system is found in the United States Constitution in Article III, section 1:

> The judicial Power of the United States shall be vested in one supreme Court, and in such inferior Courts as the Congress may from time to time ordain and establish.

This system of criminal courts handles all criminal matters under federal jurisdiction and which are not in any state's jurisdiction as set forth in the United States Constitution, Article III, section 2:

> The judicial Power shall extend to . . . all Cases affecting Ambassadors, other public Ministers and Consuls;—to all Cases of admiralty and maritime Jurisdiction; . . . —between a State and Citizens of another State;—between Citizens of different States. . . .
>
> In all Cases affecting Ambassadors, other public Ministers and Consuls, and those in which a State shall be Party, the supreme Court shall have original Jurisdiction. In all the other Cases before mentioned, the supreme Court shall have appellate Jurisdiction. . . .

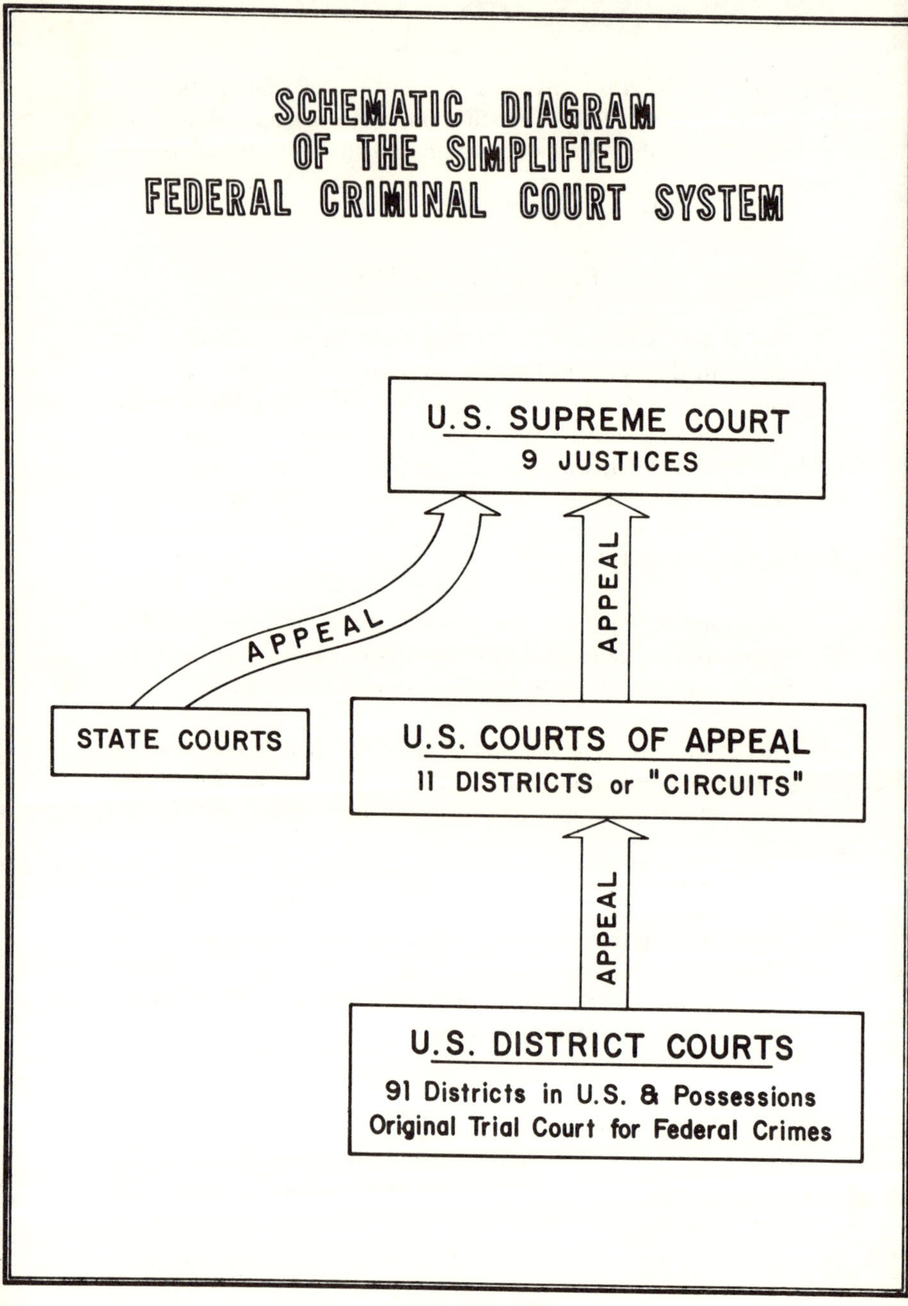
SCHEMATIC DIAGRAM
OF THE SIMPLIFIED
FEDERAL CRIMINAL COURT SYSTEM
U.S. SUPREME COURT
9 JUSTICES
APPEAL
APPEAL
STATE COURTS
U.S. COURTS OF APPEAL
11 DISTRICTS or "CIRCUITS"
APPEAL
U.S. DISTRICT COURTS
91 Districts in U.S. & Possessions
Original Trial Court for Federal Crimes

FIGURE II–2

U.S. DISTRICT COURTS

The lowest level of federal criminal courts is the District Courts level. It is at this level that all federal crimes are originally charged and tried. Within the 50 states and 5 possessions of the United States, there are 91 federal court districts, each district having one court. The districts have varying geographic extent.

Jurisdiction of these federal courts is defined in the United States Constitution under Article III, section 2. Basically, this jurisdiction covers Ambassadors, Ministers, Consuls, admiralty and maritime cases, cases involving a state and citizens of another state, and cases involving citizens of different states.

Consequently, if you commit a crime which lies outside of the jurisdictional limits of any state, but is under federal jurisdiction, you will be charged and tried in a federal district court.

Consider the following examples:

George and John, both U.S. citizens, are part of the crew of a U.S. merchant ship. While at sea in international waters, John kills George during a fight. John's trial for homicide would be held in a U.S. district court.

Frankie, being hot tempered, gets into a violent argument with a well-dressed middle aged man. During the argument, Frankie commits battery against the gentleman. Since the gentleman is an ambassador from a foreign country, Frankie's trial for criminal battery would be held in a U.S. district court.

U.S. COURTS OF APPEAL

The second level of federal courts is the U.S. courts of appeal (see Figure II–2). These are basically courts of appeal for the U.S. district courts. These are not original courts of jurisdiction in that federal crime charges are not originally brought against a suspect in these courts. The United States is divided into eleven districts each with a single court. As with the U.S. district courts, the eleven districts vary in geographical extent. Originally these districts were referred to as "circuits" and the courts as the U.S.

circuit courts; however, this terminology is now outdated somewhat.

Thus it is seen that if you commit a federal crime and are convicted in a U.S. district court, you may appeal the decision to a U.S. court of appeal.

U.S. SUPREME COURT

The ultimate court to which any federal crime may be appealed is the United States Supreme Court (see Figure II–2). It is presently composed of nine justices, appointed for life by the President of the United States. Cases which are lost on appeal to the U.S. Court of Appeal may appeal to the U.S. Supreme Court, which is the ultimate "court of last resort" in the United States. Also as mentioned in the discussion on state courts, criminal cases that lose at the state supreme court level may be appealed (but not always) to the U.S. Supreme Court (provided that a question is present which involves interpretation of some aspect of the United States Constitution).

In most instances, the Supreme Court has the right to decide which cases it will hear. The majority of cases presented for appeal from lower courts are by *writ of certiorari.* This procedure is initiated when a person convicted of a crime appeals the lower court's decision. If the U.S. Supreme Court decides to review the case, it issues a writ of certiorari which requires that the lower court provide a copy of all documents relating to the trial. After thorough review, the Court may reverse the lower court's decision or it may allow the lower court's decision to stand (remain as is). Should the Supreme Court decide not to issue a writ (that is, not to review the case), then the lower court's decision automatically remains unchanged.

Chapter 6

POLICE PROCEDURE

Now that we have discussed what law is, how it originated, what crime is, and specific crimes having some relationship to the martial arts, let us now examine the procedures the police must follow in bringing you before a court. The section is divided into two parts. The first part deals with the arrest procedure; the second part considers the post-arrest procedure. Within the topic of arrest, arrest is defined, and arrest with or without a warrant is examined. Of particular interest to the martial arts students who are police officers is the discussion of how much force may be used in the arrest. The topic of citizen's arrest and amount of force allowed in making such an arrest is valuable for the martial arts students who are not police officers. The section on post-arrest procedure discusses the "booking" process, interrogation, and the civil liability of police in making arrests.

ARREST

It is highly probable that the vast majority of martial arts students will never be arrested. However, for those few who may be arrested, the following explanations will detail both the steps which you may expect to occur and what your rights are during the arrest.

DEFINITION OF ARREST

Arrest is the act of taking some individual into legal custody with the intent that he be charged with having violated some law. As will be seen, the performance of arrest is not limited to just law enforcement officers, but also may be performed by citizens utilizing a citizen's arrest.

The suspect must be informed of the fact that he is being arrested, and the word "arrest" should be specifically used. A suggestion or invitation to go to the police station could not be construed as an arrest. Further, an attempt to arrest a person without informing him of the arrest would allow the person to actively and forcefully resist the attempt. The charge of resisting arrest can only be made against the suspect if the suspect had been informed beforehand of the arrest attempt and if the arrest is valid.

Words alone, unaccompanied by any particular physical act, are sufficient to constitute arrest. Once the words are spoken informing the suspect of the arrest, he is considered to be arrested. There need not be any physical control of the suspect whatsoever. Of course, if the suspect is considered or thought to be dangerous, he will in all probability be handcuffed immediately.

ARREST WITHOUT A WARRANT

Arrest can be performed under two situations. That is, an arrest may be made either with or without a warrant. We will examine arrest without a warrant first and then proceed to arrest with a warrant. For the time being, then, we postpone defining what a warrant is. Generally speaking, an arrest without a warrant may be performed in the event that escape of a felony suspect is imminent and probable. Additionally, in most states, an arrest without a warrant may be made for the commission of any misdemeanor. However, it is generally necessary that the misdemeanor be committed in view of the police officer to allow arrest without a warrant. Of course, a felony committed in the presence of a police officer would also allow arrest without a warrant. Finally, an arrest without a warrant may be made by a police officer for a felony that was not committed in the officer's presence; however, there are certain limitations placed on this right.

Probable Cause

If the officer is not an actual witness to the commission of a felony, he must have a strong reason for arresting the suspect without a warrant. He is required to have "probable cause." Amendment 4 of the United States Constitution states:

> . . . and no Warrants shall issue, but upon probable cause, supported by Oath or affirmation. . . .

Probable cause means having sufficient evidence such that a reasonable and prudent person could realistically suspect that the suspect had committed a felony.

Hearsay Evidence

In considering what constitutes probable cause, the question will arise of how to treat tips from informers. This is the kind of information volunteered by a person who was not an eyewitness to the commission of a felony. Such information, which borders on being a rumor, can be relied on by an officer only if he has previously received reliable tips from the informer thereby establishing him as a credible source. In cases where the informer has not yet been established as a credible source, the officer will need some additional evidence to corroborate the informant's tip.

ARREST WITH A WARRANT

The second method of performing an arrest is with a warrant. The Constitutional requirement of having a warrant to make certain arrests is a safeguard against the police abusing the arrest process.

A warrant is a written document issued by a court ordering the arrest of a specified individual. There are certain requirements that must be met in order for the warrant to be legally valid.

First, in order to initiate the issuance of a warrant, a complaint must be filed by an officer with the judge having jurisdiction over the site where the alleged felony occurred. The officer must demonstrate in the complaint that probable cause exists for making the arrest. As previously mentioned, probable cause is a body of evidence sufficient for an average reasonable person to conclude that the suspect may have committed the felony in question. Additionally, the officer must take an oath that the facts supporting probable cause are, to his knowledge, truthful.

Second, the warrant must sufficiently identify the person to be arrested to prevent a case of mistaken identity. Normally, giving the person's full name, correctly spelled, is adequate. On occasion, however, the suspect's name may not be known. In this event, sufficient physical description together with any other pertinent data must be provided to insure, as much as possible, that the correct individual is arrested. Such information, in addition to the suspect's physical description, includes his place of residence or his place of employment.

Third, the charge against the suspect must be included in the warrant. A brief statement is sufficient. The details of the charge, including the data for probable cause, are contained in the complaint, which is on record with the court.

Fourth, the warrant must be signed by the judge.

Should any of these four requirements not be fulfilled or incorrectly listed on the warrant, then the warrant may be invalid. In such an event, the suspect's attorney may free his client by filing a legal request (referred to as a "motion") to have the arrest declared illegal because of an invalid warrant.

JURISDICTION

One aspect of a valid arrest is that the arrest must be made in the jurisdiction in which the police officer is authorized to operate. The only exception to this rule is the "hot pursuit" doctrine, which allows a police officer to pursue a criminal suspect as far as necessary to arrest him—provided that the pursuit began in his own jurisdiction. Normally, then, a city police officer is restricted to making arrests only within his own city, a state police officer to making arrests only within his own state. One interesting point is that even though a police officer cannot initiate an arrest outside of his jurisdiction in his role as an officer, he can make arrests outside of his jurisdiction as a citizen. (For more detail, see the section on citizen's arrest.)

USE OF FORCE

Of interest perhaps to martial arts students (particularly those involved in law enforcement) is the amount of force that may be used by a police officer when making an arrest. (The amount of force that may be used in a citizen's arrest is discussed under the topic of citizen's arrest.) The basic guideline is that the amount of force to be used must be only that degree which is reasonable in order to safely apprehend the suspect. Under this rule, a police officer may use sufficient force to protect both himself and bystanders from bodily injury by the suspect.

"Reasonable force" cannot be defined in an absolute sense. That is, the degree of force to be used depends on the situation. Some of the factors that affect any given situation include:

1. *The type of crime.* The amount of force necessary to arrest someone committing a misdemeanor normally need not be as great as for someone committing a felony. Felonies, being serious crimes under the law, allow killing the suspect if no other alternative is available in order to apprehend him. Death is considered an unreasonable amount of force when attempting to arrest someone for a misdemeanor.

2. *The presence of assistance for the officer.* Certainly if the suspect is a small person and three brawny officers are present, beating the suspect into unconsciousness would be both unreasonable and unnecessary. In this regard, it should be noted that any police officer can request the assistance of any citizen in helping him arrest a suspect. Failure of the citizen to aid the officer is a crime. Once the citizen's assistance is requested, he has the same rights as the officer in using force. However, of immediate importance to martial arts students, is the fact that the citizen is also restricted to using a reasonable amount of force to assist the officer.

3. *Self-defense.* A police officer has the right to use a reasonable amount of force for his own self-defense if attacked. Again, the law would allow the officer to kill a felony suspect if necessary; whereas, the killing of a misdemeanor suspect who attacks the officer is normally not allowed. In some situations, however, a misdemeanor suspect may be shot in order to disable him.

The importance of this topic to the martial arts student is to demonstrate what force a police officer may use against a person either attacking him or resisting arrest. It is very difficult to imagine any situation in which a person would be allowed to use force against a police officer, even though the law allows a citizen to legally resist an unlawful arrest. The realistic aspect of using force against a police officer is to consider his point of view. He undoubtedly believes that he is doing the correct thing when arresting any individual. If a citizen resists, the officer will believe that he is justified in using force to subdue the suspect. If other officers are present, they will certainly aid their fellow officer. From a practical point of view, officers carry guns. If provoked to a certain level (such as use of extreme force against them), it is logical to expect the officer to use his gun. The theory behind a law is one thing. The realism of what will probably happen is entirely another thing. The author cautions anyone arrested to go peacefully in a cooperative manner with the arresting officer. There are legal procedures for correcting illegal arrests as discussed elsewhere in this text.

SEARCH AND SEIZURE

The Fourth Amendment of the United States Constitution states:

> The right of the people to be secure in their persons, homes, papers, and effects, against unreasonable searches and seizures, shall not be violated, and no warrants shall issue, but upon probable cause, supported by oath or affirmation, and particularly observing the place to be searched, and the persons or things to be seized.

For purposes of the martial arts, it is not necessary to discuss the complete topic of search and seizure. Only those aspects will be discussed which the author believes may have some relationship to martial arts students.

As stated here in the Fourth Amendment, citizens are protected by the law against unreasonable searches and seizures. In order for your residence or business office to be searched, a search warrant is required. A search warrant is a court issued document allowing the officer to search the premises for specified items. Usually, though, the kinds of searches a martial arts student may be faced with are of two types, neither of which requires the officer involved to have a search warrant.

The Person

The first of these searches which you may be subjected to, and the most likely, is the searching of your person associated with an arrest. The law allows an officer to search, without a warrant, a suspect in order to confiscate any items the suspect might use to harm the officer or that might be used as evidence against the suspect. Of course, this requires a valid arrest, the requirements of which have been discussed. Thus it is clearly legal for an officer to search you if you are arrested as a suspect in a crime. Additionally, if an officer has reasonable belief that you possess an illegal deadly weapon, he may search you before an arrest is made. Should the officer find a weapon, he has two choices after questioning you. He must either return the weapon (assuming you are legally entitled to carry it) and release you, or else he must keep the weapon and arrest you. An example will aid your understanding of the topic as it bears on the martial arts.

Assume that you possess a set of nunchakus and become involved in a fight with another person. During the fight, you strike your opponent with the nunchakus. An officer, arriving on the scene, after the fight has ended, determines that you were involved. Without placing you under arrest, but having good reason to suspect that you were the person possessing the weapon (which is now stuck in your belt and out of sight under your jacket), he searches you. Upon finding the weapon, and since you are in a city forbidding their possession, he arrests you.

The Car

The second type of situation in which you might be searched without a warrant involves you in your car (or in any other vehicle). The law allows a police officer to stop and search a car provided that he has reasonable evidence to provide a probable cause.

Altering the earlier example slightly will provide a second example here. Suppose that following a fight in which you strike a person with your nunchakus, you go to your car and leave the scene. Someone takes your license number and gives it to the police. Later, an officer stops you and searches your car for the weapon. Finding it under the front seat of your car, he arrests you. This is a legal search and seizure.

CITIZEN'S ARREST

One of the unique aspects of the law that many people are not aware of is the right of citizens to conduct an arrest. This right extends to arrest for both misdemeanors and felonies but may vary from state to state. Under the common law and under statutory law, a citizen is allowed to arrest a person who has committed a felony in his presence. In some states, statutory law also allows the citizen to arrest a person upon probable cause that the person either has committed, or is going to commit, a felony. In many states, there is no statutory basis for allowing a citizen to make an arrest for a misdemeanor committed in his presence. Consequently, such an arrest may not be allowable in your state.

Use of Force

The use of force in making a citizen's arrest is of significance to any martial arts student. Although the chances of your ever actually witnessing a felony being committed are quite slim, there is nevertheless a possibility. Further, among the general population, students of the martial arts have the potential to apply sufficient reasonable force to retain the suspect once a citizen's arrest is made. It is very important to understand that only a reasonable amount of force may be used to subdue the suspect if he resists the arrest.

From a practical standpoint, you should know the law of your state as it pertains to citizen's arrest. Additionally, before arresting someone for committing a felony, you must be certain that, in fact, the person's act was a felony in your state. In those states allowing arrest for a misdemeanor, you will have to know for certain that the person's act was a misdemeanor. You can well imagine the legal entanglement that could result if you attempted to arrest someone for a felony and, in fact, his actions were legal. He undoubtedly would resist your arrest in which case you would attempt to subdue him. To avoid such a hypothetical mess, be absolutely certain that you are acting appropriately before making a citizen's arrest.

POST-ARREST PROCEDURE

Now that the arrest procedure has been examined, the next process to logically discuss is the post-arrest procedures that occur. Included are the timeliness of bringing the suspect before a court subsequent to his arrest, the interrogation process, and the lineup.

DELIVERY TO COURT REQUIREMENT

Amendment 6 of the United States Constitution states:

> In all criminal prosecutions, the accused shall enjoy the right to a speedy and public trial. . . .

It is required that a police officer, subsequent to making an arrest, must bring the suspect before a court for a hearing as soon as possible and without any needless delay. From a federal standpoint, the delay may not be more than a few hours due to a Supreme Court decision. However, delay within some states may be several days. The reason for the law attempting to prevent unnecessary delay in bringing an arrested person before a court is the abuse of the person's rights which possibly could creep into the system. Some anxious police use the delay period to attempt to extract a confession from the suspect. The subject of interrogation will be discussed shortly in greater detail.

WRIT OF HABEAS CORPUS

At any point during a suspect's detention, either subsequent to arrest and before delivery to court or during the pre-trial procedures, the suspect's attorney may file for a writ of habeas corpus with the court. This legal action is a request on behalf of the defendant to have the court issue a writ of habeas corpus. The attorney makes the request and the court issues the writ. A writ of heabeas corpus is a demand by the court for the defendant to be produced in person by whomever is holding him in custody.

In the case of unnecessary delay, the police must charge the suspect with having committed a specific crime or else they must release him. The Constitution of the United States as well as the constitutions of every state provide for the right of habeas corpus. The obvious necessity for such a right is to prevent arbitrary arrest and detention by police.

BOOKING

The booking procedure is a simple process during which a suspect's name and the charge against him are entered into a "book" at the police station. Additionally, at that time, the suspect will probably be photographed and fingerprinted. Although there have been cases objecting to fingerprinting as unconstitutional, court decisions have ruled that fingerprinting of a suspect is not unconstitutional. One of the obvious reasons for fingerprinting is to allow the police to determine whether or not the suspect is wanted elsewhere for committing a crime.

INTERROGATION

The rights of a suspect during the interrogation process are extremely important. There are safeguards built into the American legal system designed to protect these rights as fully as possible.

Right to Remain Silent

One of these safeguards is the right of the suspect to remain silent during the interrogation process. This right stems from the now classic and famous U.S. Supreme Court decision in the case of Miranda v. Arizona in 1966. The decision in this case now requires police officers to warn a suspect of his Constitutional rights:

1. To remain silent.

2. Anything the suspect says can be used as evidence against him.
3. Have a right to obtain a lawyer before interrogation begins.
4. If the suspect cannot hire his own lawyer, the court will appoint one for him (at taxpayers' expense).

Right Against Coercion

A second safeguard of an arrested person's rights is that coercion of any form by the police in order to obtain a confession is forbidden and is illegal. Coercion, in this sense, includes any physical torture, any threat of physical abuse, or any kind of threat designed to frighten the suspect into confessing. Also included are any promises designed to lure the suspect into confessing. Often such promises deal with leniency of sentencing. Courts will accept only voluntary confession from defendants.

Right to Lawyer

The Miranda decision guarantees that all arrested persons are informed of their Constitutional right to have professional legal assistance before and during interrogation. Additionally, the right guarantees that the suspect is entitled to legal counsel whether or not he can afford it. Thus if a suspect cannot afford to hire an attorney, the court will appoint either a public defender or some other attorney to defend him. The presence of an attorney with the suspect during his interrogation is designed to insure that unlawful coercive methods are not used to extract a confession from the suspect. Additionally, the attorney will insure that the suspect makes no statements that might tend to incriminate himself.

Right Against Self-Incrimination

The Fifth Amendment of the United States Constitution guarantees that a criminal suspect need not say anything during his interrogation or trial which might tend to incriminate him. This Amendment states:

> No person . . . shall be compelled in any criminal case to be a witness against himself. . . .

The reasoning behind this guarantee is that the American legal system presumes that a criminal suspect is innocent until proven guilty. The burden of proving the defendant guilty rests with the state. Significantly, the state cannot force the defendant to say anything during either his interrogation or at his trial which might tend to incriminate him in having participated in the crime.

CIVIL AND CRIMINAL LIABILITY OF POLICE

Civil

What recourse do you have if the police exceed their limitations either during the arrest or detention stages? Basically, a citizen may sue for damages if his rights have been violated by a police officer. Although it is possible to sue the officer, most do not have the financial resources to pay a large damage award. Therefore, it is more likely that a person would sue the city or state in which the violation occurred.

Criminal

Although it is possible to file criminal charges against a police officer for exceeding his authority against a citizen, the reality of such a situation is against prosecution. For example, an officer can be charged with assault or battery or coercing a confession (in some states). However, in order for a court to convict a police officer on criminal charges arising from him performing his police duties, it will have to be a very strong case with very positive evidence leaving no doubt as to guilt.

Chapter 7

PRE-TRIAL PROCEDURES

Now that the arrest and initial confinement in jail procedure have been discussed, we will now examine the actual court procedures. These are the key elements of the American legal system, since the process determines a criminal suspect's guilt or innocence. The discussion will begin with pre-trial procedures.

The pre-trial procedures are those processes that occur after an arrested criminal suspect has been brought before the court, but before the actual trial procedures begin. After arrest, a suspect is brought before a judge who will conduct a preliminary hearing to determine if the suspect should be held or released. If held, bail may be set to allow temporary freedom for the suspect. If a grand jury finds that sufficient evidence exists, an indictment will be issued against the suspect. Following the grand jury indictment, the suspect will be formally arraigned before the court. Subsequent to the arraignment, the defendant's attorney will attempt one or more pre-trial motions in order to obtain the release of his client. Each of these pre-trial steps will now be discussed in more detail.

PRELIMINARY HEARING

Subsequent to arrest, the first felony pre-trial procedure that

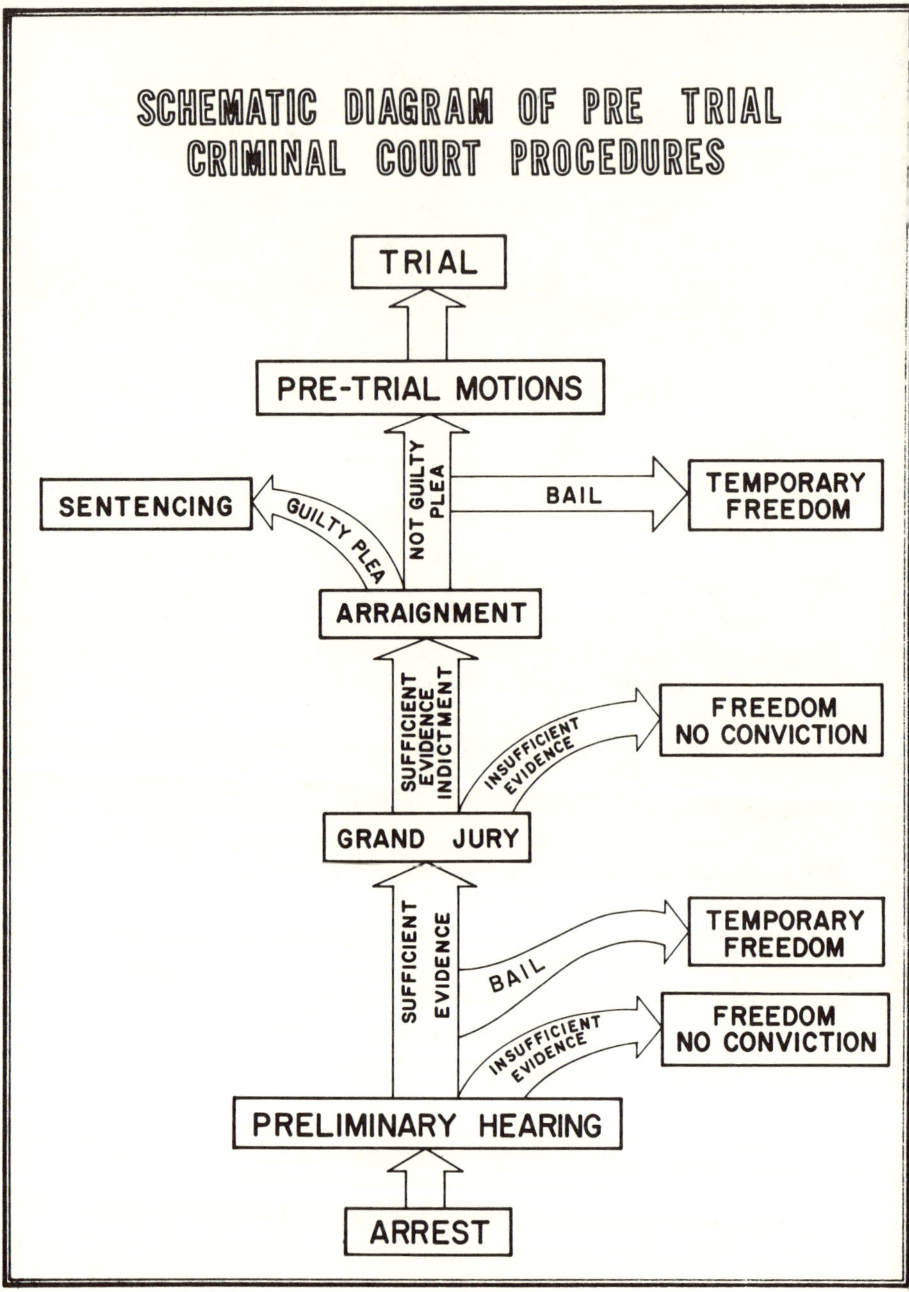
SCHEMATIC DIAGRAM OF PRE TRIAL
CRIMINAL COURT PROCEDURES
TRIAL
PRE-TRIAL MOTIONS
SENTENCING
GUILTY PLEA
NOT GUILTY PLEA
BAIL
TEMPORARY FREEDOM
ARRAIGNMENT
SUFFICIENT EVIDENCE INDICTMENT
INSUFFICIENT EVIDENCE
FREEDOM NO CONVICTION
GRAND JURY
SUFFICIENT EVIDENCE
BAIL
TEMPORARY FREEDOM
INSUFFICIENT EVIDENCE
FREEDOM NO CONVICTION
PRELIMINARY HEARING
ARREST

FIGURE II–3

occurs is the preliminary hearing. As shown in Figure II–3, the preliminary hearing stage precedes any grand jury action. At the hearing, the judge first advises the accused person of his right to have legal counsel during the hearing (unless the accused already has an attorney present with him). Under a 1963 United States Supreme Court decision (made in the case of Gideon v. Wainwright), every accused person brought before a court is entitled to legal counsel to aid him in his defense. If the accused cannot afford to hire his own attorney, then the court must provide an attorney for him free of charge. The Supreme Court decision is actually an amplification of the Sixth Amendment to the United States Constitution:

> In all criminal prosecutions, the accused shall enjoy the right . . . to have the Assistance of Counsel for his defense.

Generally such a court-appointed attorney is obtained from the public defender's office. In some states, a local attorney is appointed at the judge's discretion to defend the accused.

If the accused is appointed a court attorney, the judge will, in all likelihood, postpone further proceedings in the hearing for several days in order to give the newly appointed attorney time to prepare a defense. At this time, the judge may set bail for the accused thereby granting him temporary freedom until the hearing resumes at a later date. Bail is a financial guarantee by the accused deposited with the court offering some strong degree of assurance that the accused will return to the court on an appointed date. The amount of bail set by the court varies with the seriousness of the offense and also varies from state to state. The right to bail is discussed in more detail later.

Upon resumption of the preliminary hearing several days later, the judge listens to all the evidence presented by the prosecuting attorney, the arresting officer(s), the defense attorney, the defendant, and witnesses. It should be noted that during the hearing, the defendant is not required to make any statement to the court. As shown in Figure II–4, if the accused had originally been present at the preliminary hearing with his hired attorney having prepared the defense case, the hearing would not have been postponed and would have been completed in one session, rather than the two required for a court appointed attorney.

In either case, whether hired attorney or court appointed attorney, the moment arrives when the judge has heard all the evidence presented by both the prosecution and the defense. The judge then decides whether or not he believes sufficient evidence is present to justify presenting the case to the grand jury for its consideration.

Should the judge decide that the evidence presented indicates insufficient facts to prove the accused committed any crime, he may release the suspect from further custody. At this point, then, the suspect is granted his freedom. However should additional evidence against the suspect become available to the court, the grand jury may still return an indictment against the suspect at some later date.

On the other hand, if the judge does decide that reasonable evidence is present to indicate a strong probability of the suspect's guilt, then the case will be sent to the grand jury. The accused will be bound over (retained in custody by the court) for the grand jury's decision. Of course, at this point, the accused person has not been found guilty by the court. The preliminary hearing is a preliminary "screening" process whereby the court makes its first examination of the evidence in the case. Doubtful cases are rejected; whereas, probable cases are accepted for further court examination.

THE RIGHT TO BAIL

Figures II–3 and II–4 demonstrate that at this point in the criminal court procedure, the judge may grant the accused temporary freedom by setting bail. Amendment 8 to the United States Constitution guarantees the right to bail by stating:

> Excessive bail shall not be required . . .

Bail is a financial deposit which the defendant makes with

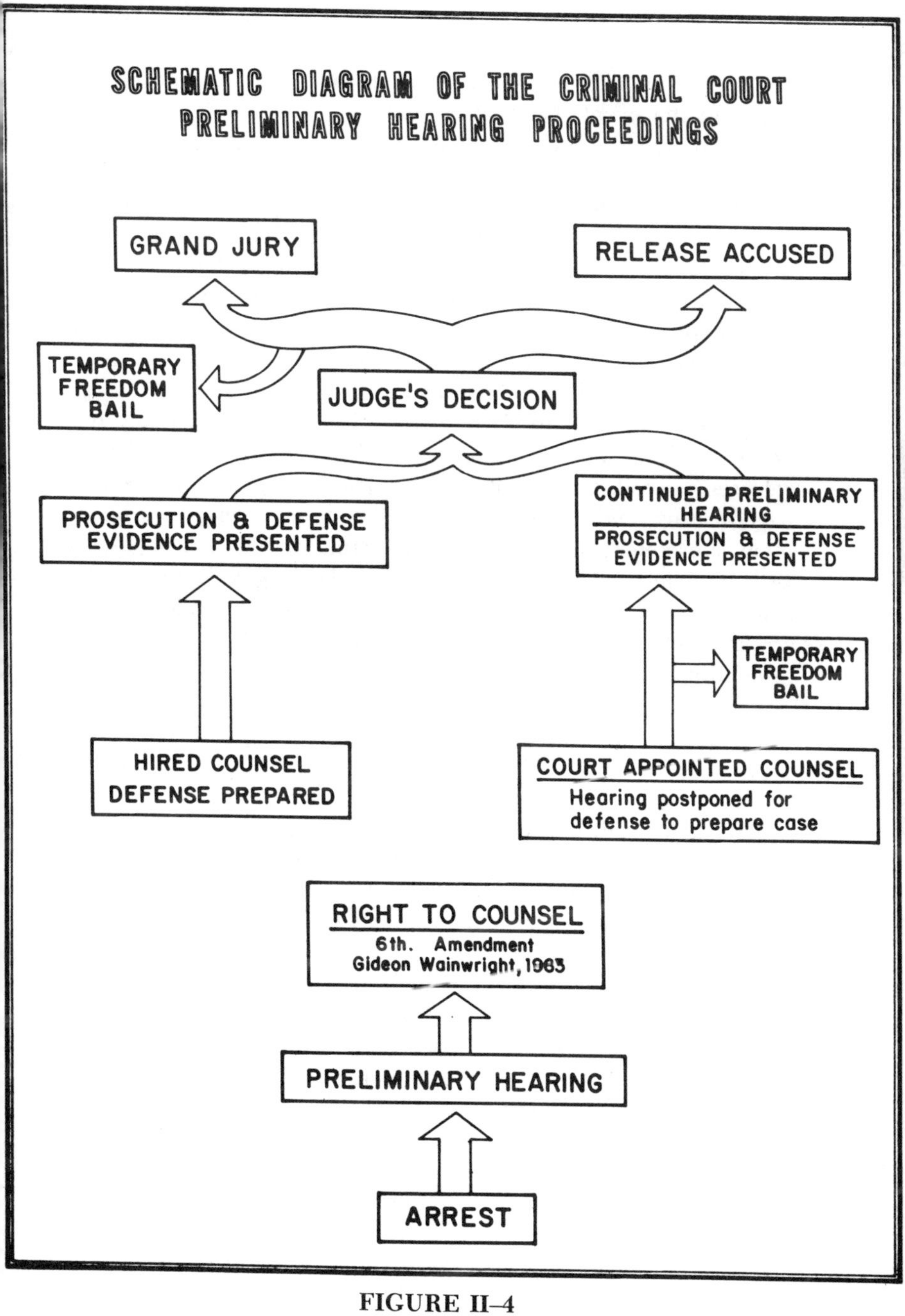
SCHEMATIC DIAGRAM OF THE CRIMINAL COURT PRELIMINARY HEARING PROCEEDINGS
GRAND JURY
RELEASE ACCUSED
TEMPORARY FREEDOM BAIL
JUDGE'S DECISION
PROSECUTION & DEFENSE EVIDENCE PRESENTED
CONTINUED PRELIMINARY HEARING
PROSECUTION & DEFENSE EVIDENCE PRESENTED
TEMPORARY FREEDOM BAIL
HIRED COUNSEL DEFENSE PREPARED
COURT APPOINTED COUNSEL
Hearing postponed for defense to prepare case
RIGHT TO COUNSEL
6th. Amendment
Gideon Wainwright, 1963
PRELIMINARY HEARING
ARREST

FIGURE II–4

the court to guarantee that he will return to court at a designated time. In the event that he fails to return, the bail is forfeited to the court. Once the bail is paid the defendant is granted temporary freedom.

Usually a defendant cannot afford to put up the entire amount of bail himself. In many cases, therefore, a defendant will obtain the bail money from a bail bondsman in the form of a loan. Payment to the bondsman is often a small percentage of the gross amount of bail. In some cases, the committed crime may have been of such a vicious nature that the court will not allow the accused person out of custody on bail.

Referring to Figure II–3, notice that there are actually two points in the court procedure where the accused person may be released on bail. One point is immediately following the preliminary hearing, and the other is immediately following the arraignment subsequent to a grand jury indictment. The bail deposited with the court following the preliminary hearing will probably be sufficient to allow the defendant temporary freedom following the arraignment. That is to say, the defendant would not be required to deposit two separate bails for the same crime.

THE GRAND JURY

If, as a result of the preliminary hearing, the judge has decided that there is sufficient evidence to indicate that the accused did commit a crime, then the case is brought before the grand jury. Amendment 5 of the United States Constitution states:

> No person shall be held to answer for a capital, or otherwise infamous crime, unless on a presentment or indictment of a Grand Jury, except in cases arising in the land or naval forces, or in the Militia, when in actual service in time of War or public danger. . . .

The grand jury is not a trial jury. That is, its members do not attempt to determine the guilt or innocence of the defendant. It is the function of this jury to determine whether or not a minimum level of evidence exists sufficient to establish a reasonable belief that the accused did commit a crime.

Grand jury consideration of the evidence in felony cases is required in a number of states. The usual number of jury members is 23 with 16 constituting a quorum. Twelve members must vote for charging the accused with a felony crime in order to deliver an indictment against the accused. An indictment is also referred to as a true bill.

One significant aspect of grand jury proceedings is that only the prosecuting attorney (often the district attorney) is allowed to present evidence against the defendant. The defense attorney is not allowed to present evidence in favor of the defendant before the grand jury. Additionally, only very rarely is the defendant allowed to personally appear before the grand jury.

Although this may seem inherently unfair and onesided, keep in mind that this is not a trial jury. The grand jury is simply another screening stage along the defendant's path to trial. Just as the judge at the preliminary hearing determines initially if sufficient evidence exists for believing the accused committed a crime, the grand jury likewise makes a similar determination. In effect, the grand jury is an independent system that verifies or overrules the preliminary hearing judge's decision.

If the grand jury finds that insufficient evidence exists to charge the accused with having committed a crime, then a no bill is returned. This means that the court must release the suspect due to lack of adequate justification to further detain him. He is not necessarily permanently free, however. Should further evidence come to the grand jury's attention, an indictment may be returned against the accused at some later date.

THE ARRAIGNMENT

Should the grand jury return an indictment, or true bill, against the accused, then the defendant will be brought before the court for arraignment. This is a formal pleading process for the accused person. The process begins with the defendant being brought before the court. Then the presiding judge (who is a different judge from the preliminary hearing judge) reads the indictment to the defendant thereby fully advising him of the charges against him. According to Amendment 6 of the United States Constitution:

> In all criminal prosecutions, the accused shall enjoy the right . . . to be informed of the nature and cause of the accusation. . . .

Of course, throughout the arraignment proceeding, the defendant will be accompanied by his legal counsel, whether hired attorney or court appointed attorney.

Subsequent to reading the indictment, the judge will ask how the defendant wishes to plead to the charges against him. The defendant's plea may be entered by either himself personally or else by his attorney acting on the defendant's behalf. The defendant has several choices of pleas available to him at this point:

1. He may plead "guilty."
2. He may plead "not guilty."
3. He may plead "nolo contendere."
4. He may request additional time before making his plea.
5. He may move to set aside the indictment.
6. He may demur to the charge.

If the defendant's plea is guilty, then no trial is necessary. Since a trial is held only when it is necessary to determine a person's guilt, the admission of guilt eliminates the need for a trial. The judge can, therefore, proceed with sentencing of the defendant.

Should the defendant plead not guilty to the charges brought against him by the grand jury indictment, then a trial will be necessary. The trial procedure will be discussed in the next section. At this point, the judge may grant temporary freedom to the accused by setting bail (previously discussed).

The defendant can plead nolo contendere, although this plea is allowed only for lesser criminal offenses and not for felony cases. Basically, the plea means that the accused is neither admitting nor denying guilt, but he does not want to have a trial. In effect, he is willing to take whatever punishment (usually a fine) the judge sentences him to.

If the defendant's attorney does not consider that his case for the defense is adequately prepared at this time, then he may request additional time to study the case. The attorney's purpose is to determine the best plea for his client to make.

There often is a considerable amount of behind-the-scenes bargaining that occurs between the prosecuting attorney and the defense attorney. This is particularly true of public defenders and other court appointed attorneys having heavy case loads. There is nothing illegal about the bargaining. In fact, the process is somewhat of a necessity in order for the court system to function in the face of the tremendous number of criminal cases to be handled by most criminal courts. The result of the bargaining process often seems to be to the benefit of the defendant.

Should the defense attorney believe that some irregularity has occurred during his client's arrest, detention, interrogation, obtaining of confession, preliminary hearing, etc., he may make a motion that the grand jury indictment be set aside for the specified reason he offers. Such a maneuver often fails, but it nevertheless offers another safeguard to the defendant's right in the event that some significant violation of his rights has occurred.

Finally, the defendant or his attorney has the choice when pleading of demurring to the charge. This plea is actually a motion which claims that the defendant has been subjected to an incorrect, improper, or invalid charge. The actual effect of this plea is to forestall any further action by the court against the defendant. This is due to the fact that no further consideration of the defendant's guilt or innocence can be made until the judge issues a ruling on the demurrer. In truth, the majority of such pleas are ruled against by the presiding judge; but, nevertheless, they provide another safeguard to the defendant's Constitutional rights during criminal court proceedings.

PRE-TRIAL MOTIONS

Following the arraignment, should the defendant plead not guilty, the presiding judge will set a trial date. Prior to the trial, however, the defense attorney may attempt to interrupt or end the court procedures through the filing of one or more pretrial motions:

1. Motion for a change of venue.
2. Motion to suppress unconstitutionally obtained evidence.
3. Motion to quash the indictment.

Since the term "venue" means "location," change of venue means changing the site of the trial from the court having jurisdiction where the alleged crime occurred. The defense attorney especially will attempt to obtain a change of venue if he believes that excessive prejudice or bias exists against his client in the community at large. This type of prejudice usually occurs in cases of more serious or bizarre nature such that the various news media widely publicize the facts of the case. This obviously would make it difficult to select an unbiased jury.

The motion to suppress unconstitutionally obtained evidence is another, and obvious, safeguard to the Constitutional rights of the accused. Amendment 4 of the U.S. Constitution states that:

> The right of the people to be secure in their persons, houses, papers, and effects, against unreasonable searches and seizures, shall not be violated. . . .

The legal composition of a warrant as well as the legal process of search and seizure have been discussed earlier as separate topics. It was stated earlier, however, that during a search under a warrant when looking for specific evidence for a specific crime, evidence related to a possibly unknown and separate crime cannot be confiscated and later used in court against the defendant.

The motion to quash a grand jury indictment is an attempt by the defense attorney to claim that the indictment is based on inadequate legal basis. If the presiding judge rules favorably for the motion, then the accused gains semi-acquittal. Unfortunately, the prosecuting attorney may obtain another indictment. In effect, then, the motion to quash the indictment may only amount to a stalling action.

Chapter 8

TRIAL

If the charges against the defendant are maintained against him throughout the pre-trial procedure and the various safeguards of his Constitutional rights have assured the validity of the court procedures, then the critical and all-important trial stage is reached. As earlier discussed, the trial by jury was a most significant stage in the development of the common law in England. The trial allows the defendant to be judged by a group of his peers in an unbiased manner. It is, in fact, a Constitutional right that a defendant is entitled to a speedy and impartial trial as stated in Amendment 6 of the United States Constitution:

> In all criminal prosecutions, the accused shall enjoy the right to a speedy and public trial, by an impartial jury of the State and district wherein the crime shall have been committed and to be informed of the nature and cause of the accusation; to be confronted with the witnesses against him; to have compulsory process for obtaining witnesses in his favor, and to have the assistance of counsel for his defense.

This Amendment seems to be an amplification of Article II, section 2 of the U.S. Constitution which states:

> Trial of all crimes . . . shall be by Jury.

Of particular note within the 6th Amendment is the guarantee of a "speedy" trial. This right is further supported by legislation in each of the 50 states in order to insure that no criminal suspect is unduly detained in custody proior to his trial. (Of course, an additional safeguard against such unreasonable detention in jail is the right to bail for most criminal offenses.) Often the state statutes or constitutional guarantees provide a time limit within which the defendant's trial must be initiated. An important provision of these statutes is that their violation will result in the mandatory release of the defendant and the granting to him of permanent immunity from any subsequent prosecution for that alleged crime. The right to a speedy trial is another of the Constitutional safeguards designed to protect the rights of the accused in a criminal case.

THE JURY

The initial stage in the trial process is the selection of a jury. This section will discuss the eligibility criteria for jury duty and how the selection procedure operates in the courtroom. Additionally, the three main types of juries will be described. In a criminal trial, however, only the petit, or trial, jury is of importance, the other two juries (grand jury and coroner's jury) having functions other than trying defendants accused of crime. In the courtroom process, it is the function of the trial jury to determine the facts of the case; whereas, the presiding judge interprets the law as it pertains to the case.

ELIGIBILITY FOR JURY DUTY

Figure II–5 demonstrates that when the defendant enters a not guilty plea at his arraignment, the presiding judge sets a date for the trial to begin. The next step is selection of the jury.

A list of eligible jurors is compiled (usually on a countywide basis) from the county tax records, from the list of registered vot-

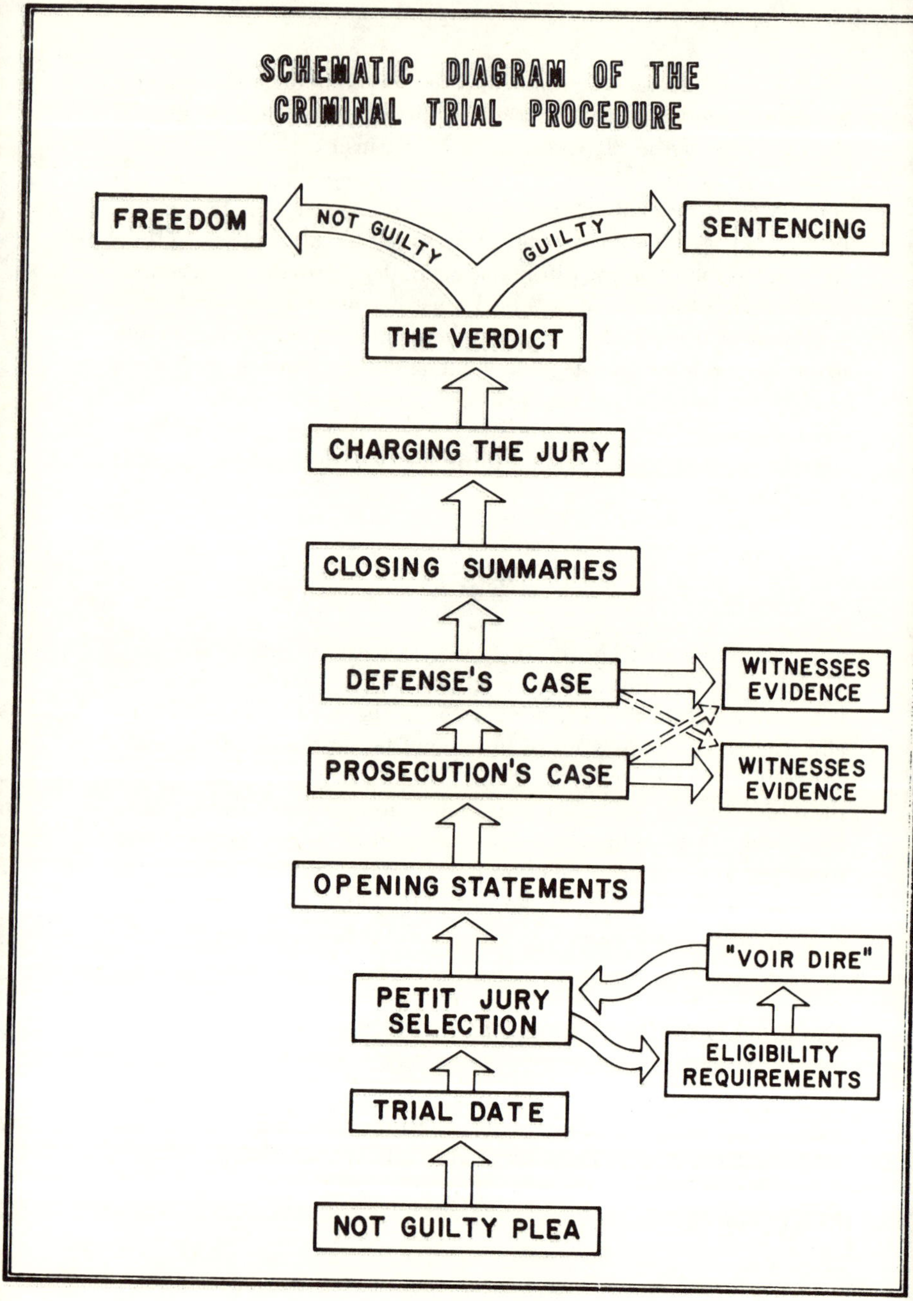
SCHEMATIC DIAGRAM OF THE
CRIMINAL TRIAL PROCEDURE
FREEDOM
NOT GUILTY
GUILTY
SENTENCING
THE VERDICT
CHARGING THE JURY
CLOSING SUMMARIES
DEFENSE'S CASE
WITNESSES
EVIDENCE
PROSECUTION'S CASE
WITNESSES
EVIDENCE
OPENING STATEMENTS
"VOIR DIRE"
PETIT JURY
SELECTION
ELIGIBILITY
REQUIREMENTS
TRIAL DATE
NOT GUILTY PLEA

FIGURE II–5

ers, or simply from a list of residents. For each trial that is scheduled to be held, a roster of perhaps 50–70 potential jurors is chosen at random from the eligibility list. Each prospective juror is then mailed a summons requiring him or her to appear for jury duty at a specified time. Failure to appear for jury duty will result in the judge issuing a bench warrant for the citizen's arrest. If the citizen lacks adequate reason for his absence, he may well be charged with a misdemeanor and fined. In addition to being either a registered voter or a property owner in order to be selected for jury duty, other eligibility requirements include:

1. United States citizenship. Registered aliens or foreign citizens residing in the U.S. on visas may not be jurors.
2. 21 years of age or older. Although the minimum voting age has been lowered to 18 in some states, the right to jury duty has not yet been made available to anyone under 21.
3. No record of felony convictions. This is not a requirement in all states. Conviction of having committed misdemeanors has no effect on eligibility for jury duty.
4. Good health, both physically and mentally. Obviously, a sickly person or a mentally unstable individual could not be depended on to make a reliable juror having reasonable and unbiased judgment.
5. Literate. The ability to read, write, and speak English is required.
6. Length of residency. Frequently there is a requirement that the prospective juror must have permanently resided in the county for a stipulated minimum length of time, ranging from 6 months to 1 year.

SELECTION PROCEDURE

The panel of prospective jurors present in the court who have met the eligibility requirements are known as veniremen. On the day of the trial, the veniremen are seated in the courtroom. Selection of the trial jury is then conducted by both the prosecuting and defending attorneys, with the trial judge overseeing the process. This selection process is referred to as the voir dire (a French expression meaning truthfulness).

The attorneys question the prospective jurors one at a time

with the objective of determining the citizen's suitability to serve on the jury as an unbiased or unprejudiced juror. There are several methods of objection to the selection of a particular juror available to the attorneys.

Peremptory Challenges

Each attorney has a limited number of peremptory challenges which he may invoke to object to certain veniremen sitting on the jury. Such challenges may be used at the discretion of either attorney and require no explanation to the judge or opposition for their use. Sometimes during the questioning of a prospective juror, the attorney will perhaps sense a bias or prejudice on the part of the venireman to the case or the defendant. Yet the bias may not be so specific that the attorney can define it to the court. Such a detection sense is acquired through experience. Although the court system allows such objections, they are limited to 10 to 20, depending on the state, for each attorney in order to prevent abuse of the process. These are obviously very open-ended challenges.

Challenges for Cause

Of a more specific nature are the challenges for cause. These are not arbitrary in nature; rather, in order for the court to recognize them, there must be definite justification for the challenges. There are two basic types of cause:

1. *General.* A general challenge for cause is made when the objecting attorney has reason to believe that the prospective juror does not meet all of the legal eligibility requirements previously discussed.
2. *Particular.* A particular challenge for cause may be of two types. First, actual bias exists when the venireman is predisposed to the defendant's guilt or innocence. Such an opinion may be due to adverse publicity of the case, racial

bias, some event in the juror's past, etc. Second, implied bias exists when the venireman has some relationship to either the defense or the prosecution. This relationship may be due to the citizen's previous jury duty in another trial at which one of the attorneys was active. There may be a social relationship between the venireman and one of the attorneys.

Eventually the jurors necessary for the trial are selected. The usual number of actual jurors required is 12 although 1 or 2 alternate jurors may also be selected. In the event that a regular juror becomes ill or dies, then an alternate juror may take his place without the court having to declare a new trial.

TYPES OF JURY

At this point, the logical sequence of discussing criminal courtroom procedures will be interrupted to explain the differences between the three principal types of juries. The jury selection process just discussed is for a petit jury (or trial jury). The function of the grand jury in indicting defendants for criminal offenses was earlier related. The third type of jury to mention is the coroner's jury, which investigates homicides and deaths due to questionable causes.

Petit Jury

The petit jury is the primary trial jury for criminal cases at the state level and at the federal level. There are 12 jurors in all petit juries, except in some municipal courts there may be only 6 jurors. As stated previously, some courts may additionally select a few (normally 3 or less) alternate jurors to replace any regular juror unable to continue during the trial. These alternates attend the complete trial just as do the regular jurors; however, the alternates have no vote in determining the final verdict unless they have replaced a regular juror during the trial.

The purpose of a petit, or trial, jury is to determine the facts in a criminal case. It has long been accepted under the English legal system that 12 heads are not only better than 1 for such a purpose, but the odds are greatly improved that the verdict will be truly fair and just.

The process through which evidence is presented by opposing sides for the jury's consideration is known as adversary pleading. In a criminal case, the "state" (meaning any governmental unit) attempts, through the prosecuting attorney (the district attorney at the county level), to prove that the defendant has committed a crime against the state. On the other hand, the defense attorney (who may be hired by the defendant or appointed by the court) attempts to prove that the defendant is innocent of having committed the charged crime.

It is for the benefit of the jury that the opposing attorneys present evidence and witnesses favoring their side of the case. Upon completion of all evidence presentation and testimony by both sides of the case, the jury must decide whether the preponderance of facts indicates the defendant's innocence or guilt.

The trial judge does not establish facts in a trial by jury; rather, he interprets the law as it pertains to the case. He is also responsible for maintaining order during the trial. Thus in a petit jury trial, the jury determines facts and the judge determines law.

Grand Jury

Although the grand jury was previously discussed in the chapter on pre-trial procedures, a brief review will be presented here of the grand jury's function and composition.

The grand jury differs from a petit jury in that a grand jury is not a trial jury. A grand jury makes no determination of innocence or guilt; rather, its purpose, in relation to criminal cases, is to evaluate the evidence presented to it by the prosecuting attorney. If it is determined that sufficient evidence exists to establish probable cause, then the grand jury will "hand down" (deliver) an indictment (or true bill) charging the defendant with having committed a specific crime. Twelve members, which represents a majority of the 23-member jury, must vote for the indictment in order for the defendant to be charged.

Most states require grand jury consideration for all felony cases; whereas, grand jury action is not required for misdemeanors.

Another difference between the petit jury and the grand jury is that grand jury proceedings are secret and not of public record; whereas, trial jury proceedings are open to the publc.

It should be noted that the grand jury is not restricted to considering only the evidence presented to it by the prosecutor. Other potential crime matters, particularly concerning governmental and other public officials, may be investigated by the grand jury if sufficient justification is present.

Coroner's Jury

A coroner's jury is dissimilar to a petit jury in that a coroner's jury is not a trial jury. It is similar to a grand jury in the sense that the jury attempts to evaluate evidence in order to determine if a crime has been committed and by whom.

The coroner is an elected or appointed official who investigates homicides, to determine whether their cause is intentional, accidental, or unknown. The jury of 6 to 12 members is chosen by the coroner or his representative (a deputy).

Unlike a grand jury, the verdict of a coroner's jury does not commit the prosecutor to proceed with a case against a defendant. The verdict of the coroner's jury is more like advice being offered to the prosecutor who may then do as he wishes with the information. Of course, a grand jury is not bound to abide the findings of a coroner's jury either. Should sufficient evidence become available, the grand jury may hand down an indictment charging a suspect with having committed a homicide.

OPENING STATEMENTS

To return now to the order in which criminal court procedures occur, Figure II–5 shows that following selection of the trial jury, opening statements are made by both the prosecuting attorney and the defense attorney. The purpose of the attorneys making opening statements is to provide the jury with a condensed outline of their respective sides of the case. The content of their statements is in the order in which they intend to present their case and includes the evidence and witnesses they intend to present to the jury. Additionally, and perhaps most important, the attorneys state exactly what they intend to prove in their cases. Without such a frame of reference, of course, the jury would have no idea of the significance of evidence or witnesses being presented. In effect, the opening statements are a preview of what is to come in the trial.

PROSECUTION'S CASE

Figure II–5 shows that following the opening statements by both attorneys, the prosecuting attorney (possibly the district attorney) presents his entire case. This means that he must present all of the evidence and testimony by witnesses, under direct examination, which he outlined in his opening statement. The prosecution is allowed to present its entire case before the defense can present its case to the jury. However, the defense attorney is not required to remain silent throughout the prosecution's case.

When the prosecution completes the presentation of testimony from a witness, the defense attorney has the opportunity to cross-examine the witness. The defense attorney is, however, restricted as to what items he may question the witness about. The cross-examination questioning may pertain to only the issues which the witness testified on. Subsequent to the cross-examination, the prosecuting attorney may return to the witness for additional questioning under redirect examination. It is very important to note that the prosecution cannot compel the defendant to testify.

In order for the prosecuting attorney to win his case, he must prove beyond a reasonable doubt that the defendant did, in fact, commit the crime with which he was charged. Should the prosecution's case have any weakness that leaves any doubt in the jurors' minds about the defendant's guilt, then the defendant will be found not guilty and set free. In fact, if the prosecution's case is too weak, the presiding judge may hand down a directed verdict of acquittal with no further trial necessary. (On the other hand, if the prosecution's case is very strong, the judge is never allowed to issue a directed verdict of guilty.)

WITNESSES

At this point, it will be worthwhile to examine the role of witnesses in a trial more closely. In any criminal trial, there may be testimony offered from two different categories of witnesses—trial witnesses and expert witnesses.

Trial Witnesses

A trial witness is one presented by either the prosecuting attorney or the defense attorney and who has some direct knowledge about the facts of the case. All witnesses are required to testify "under oath" which means they "swear to tell the truth, the whole truth, and nothing but the truth." Should a witness not tell the truth when testifying under oath, he may be found guilty of perjury (an offense punishable by fine and/or jail).

When a witness is seated to testify, it does not mean that he is free to "speak his mind" about anything and everything. He is, in fact, required to testify only about the facts, of which he has knowledge, that pertain to the case. He is not allowed to speculate on, or interpret, the value or meaning of the facts. Nor may he offer rumors or hearsay gossip as evidence. The testimony of a witness actually takes the form of direct factual answers to questions directed at the witness either by the prosecuting attorney or by the defense attorney.

Expert Witnesses

An expert witness is a person who has specialized knowledge about some item or issue directly involved in the trial. However, he does not have any knowledge relating to the facts of the case. An expert witness is also required to testify under oath.

An expert witness differs from a trial witness in that whereas the trial witness may not give his opinion on anything during his testimony, the expert witness is urged to give his opinion on matters concerned with his field of specialty. In the martial arts, it would be possible for a student who is a defendant in a criminal case involving self-defense to use his instructor as an expert witness. Other special fields requiring expert testimony include ballistics and fingerprints.

DEFENSE'S CASE

Following presentation of the prosecution's case, the defense attorney presents his case. As does the prosecution, the defense can present evidence and testimony of witnesses to support the defendant's case. If necessary, expert witnesses can be called to testify. After the defense conducts its direct examination of a witness, the prosecution has the right to cross-examine the witness.

It is not necessary that the defendant testify on his own behalf. Should the defense attorney consider it best not to use the defendant's testimony, no prejudice should exist against the defendant. In a number of states, the prosecuting attorney is not allowed to point out to the jury that the defendant did not testify. Human nature being what it is, were the refusal of the defendant to testify be pointed out, some jurors might interpret this to mean that the defendant had something to hide and therefore is guilty. The judge, when charging the jury, prior to their determining a verdict, in many states may not mention the refusal of the defendant to testify.

CLOSING SUMMARIES

The next step in the trial process, after the presentation of the defense evidence and testimony, is the presentation of closing summaries (see Figure II–5). Both the defense attorney and the prosecuting attorney summarize their cases by briefly outlining the evidence and witness testimony they have presented. Most importantly, they state to the jury what they have attempted to prove about the defendant's alleged criminal act.

The defense attorney is allowed to present his closing summary first. One of the items he will definitely make an issue of is the fact that the prosecution did not, in his opinion, establish the defendant's guilt beyond a reasonable doubt.

INSTRUCTING THE JURY

The judge gives instructions and guidance to the jury prior to the jury's retirement to the jury room to determine a verdict. This is referred to as "charging the jury." Figure II–5 shows that the jury determines the verdict on the defendant's guilt or innocence subsequent to having heard all the evidence and testimony presented by both the prosecution and the defense.

The purpose of the judge's instructions to the jury is to explain the law as it applies to the case. It is the jury's task to consider all of the facts that were presented to them and then to decide whether or not there is sufficient evidence to establish the defendant's guilt beyond a reasonable doubt.

Prior to the judge instructing the jury, both the prosecuting and defending attorneys have the right to submit instructions to the jury, which they think should be included in the judge's explanation. The judge must be careful to include these submitted instructions in his explanation to the jury, because the omission of an instruction submitted by one of the attorneys can result in a later appeal for a mistrial by the attorney. The judge not only instructs the jury orally, but also he presents the jury with written copies of his instructions in order to prevent any misunderstanding or confusion on the part of the jurors.

THE VERDICT

Following the charging of the jury by the presiding judge, the jury adjourns to the juryroom to determine their verdict for the case. The juryroom is a special room adjacent to the courtroom reserved for the use of the jury. No one is allowed inside during the jury's deliberations. Only the 12 regular jurors decide the verdict. The alternate jurors, if any, may not participate in the verdict decision unless they have been designated as a replacement for a regular juror at some point during the trial.

It is usually up to the jury to choose a foreman from among its members. The foreman's task is severalfold. First, he presides over the jury's determination of the verdict, tallying the guilty and not guilty votes during the voting. A verdict requires a unanimous vote by the jury. When a unanimous vote is finally obtained, another of the foreman's tasks is to deliver a written note to the bailiff informing the judge that a verdict has been reached.

The judge asks the jury to return to the courtroom and asks the foreman for the verdict. The foreman then announces the verdict. At this point, if the defendant has been found guilty, the judge will probably adjourn the trial for several days to further consider the case before passing sentence. If, on the other hand, the defendant has been found innocent, then the judge will order him released.

Sometimes a jury cannot reach a unanimous verdict due to opposing and unyielding opinions among the jurors. This is known as a hung jury. In such a case, the judge has no choice but to declare a mistrial. At the same time, he will set a date for a new trial which will, of course, involve selecting a new jury.

POST-CONVICTION PRE-SENTENCING PROCEDURES

Once the trial has ended and the defendant has been found guilty by the jury, the criminal court procedures available to the defendant have not yet been exhausted. This section will discuss two of the more significant alternatives yet available to the defendant and his attorney prior to sentencing by the judge. These include motion for a new trial and, motion in arrest of judgement.

MOTION FOR A NEW TRIAL

The defense attorney has the right to make a motion for a new trial, although there is usually a time limit (several days) within which the motion must be made. Normally such a maneuver by the defense attorney is based on some irregularity or technicality that he noted during the trial which he believes warrants a new and fair trial for his client. Several of these technicalities include:

1. New evidence that developed subsequent to the verdict being passed by the jury.
2. Lack of evidence which the defense believes has resulted in a case too weak to have convicted his client under the requirement of "reasonable doubt". (This requirement means that if there can be a reasonable doubt as to the defendant's guilt, then he must be acquitted.)
3. Court error in not allowing the cross-examination of a prosecution witness.
4. A biased remark made to the jury by some court employee or official.
5. Discussion of the case outside of the courtroom with a nonjuror prior to rendering the final verdict.

MOTION IN ARREST OF JUDGMENT

In the previous motion, the defense attorney was looking for a technicality occuring during the trial which he could observe and make note of. In the motion in arrest of judgment, The attorney is looking for a technicality within the court record. This is the kind of error that can be easily demonstrated to exist as it is in the court record of the proceedings against the defendant.

Should the motions be overruled by the judge, then he will set a date for sentencing the defendant. It should be noted here that at this point the court may handle the defendant in one of several ways:

1. The defendant, if previously released on bail, may be released under the same original bail.
2. The court may require the defendant to post a new bail prior to his release.
3. The court may order the accused held in jail allowing no release under bail.

SENTENCING

GENERAL

On the appointed date, the defendant and his attorney reappear in court for sentencing of the defendant (see Figure II–6). For all criminal offenses, whether state or federal, there are statutory limitations on the penalty which the judge may assess the defendant. Amendment 8 of the United States Constitution states:

> Excessive bail shall not be required, nor excessive fines imposed, nor cruel and unusual punishments inflicted.

As a result of this amendment, penalty for commission of crimes is restricted to fines and/or imprisonment with capital punishment reserved for only the most serious offenses.

For most crimes, the judge will set the sentence for the convicted person. However, many states require that the jury de-

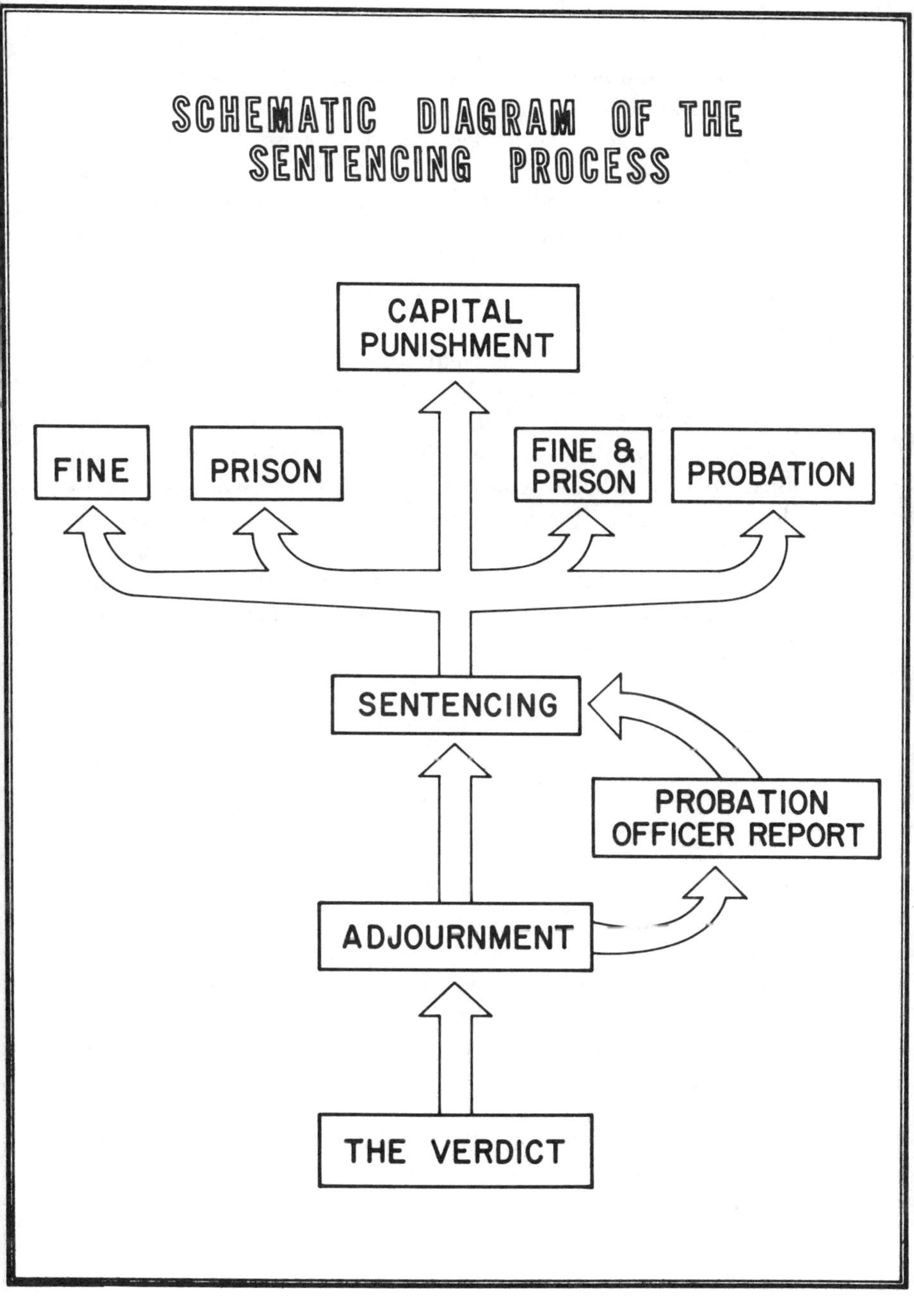
SCHEMATIC DIAGRAM OF THE SENTENCING PROCESS
CAPITAL PUNISHMENT
FINE
PRISON
FINE & PRISON
PROBATION
SENTENCING
PROBATION OFFICER REPORT
ADJOURNMENT
THE VERDICT

FIGURE II–6

termine the sentence (as well as the verdict) for persons convicted of rape or murder.

To assist the judge in deciding on what severity or leniency to adopt in passing sentence, during the adjournment period between the determination of the verdict and the passing of sentence, the convicted person's record is investigated. This is a task of the court's probation officer. He summarizes the person's criminal record (if there is one) and makes his sentencing recommendations to the judge.

Some felony offenses require, by statute, a minimum–maximum prison sentence. By this is meant a prison sentence stated as "3 to 5 years" or "4 to 7 years," etc. The smaller number refers to the minimum number of years in prison which must be served before consideration for parole will be made by the parole board. (Parole is discussed in the section on post-conviction procedures.) The larger number refers to the maximum term of years to be served for the offense. If the prisoner shows lack of good behavior, it is doubtful that the parole board would grant him early parole release.

PROBATION

Should the defendant's record be good and his present circumstances indicate a reasonable probability that he is trustworthy not to commit another crime, the judge may be allowed by statute for some crimes to place the defendant on probation. This allows the convicted individual to go free, although he is not acquitted of the crime, but he remains under the supervision of the court. The term of supervision by a probation officer may vary from 6 months to 5 years depending on the state and the seriousness of the offense. Probation requirements usually include regular visits to the probation officer by the convicted person to report on his present circumstances and activities. Additionally, the convicted person must maintain good behavior during his probation with no further criminal convictions. Should the defendant violate the conditions of his probation at any time, the court can sentence him to a prison term just as if he were originally sentenced from a trial.

POST-SENTENCING PROCEDURES

Subsequent to being sentenced to a prison term, the accused has four alternative procedures that he and his attorney may consider in order to either cancel or lessen the severity of the sentence. These alternatives are:

1. Appeal.
2. Parole.
3. Commutation.
4. Pardon.

APPEAL

The process of appeal basically means an attempt by the defense attorney to get a higher appellate court to reverse the decision of the lower court which has found his client guilty. Figures II–1 and II–2 illustrate the various appeal court levels for both state and federal criminal courts. The appellate court will thoroughly review the record of the case including the opening statements, witness testimony, cross-examination, and closing arguments. The decision of the appellate court whether to uphold or reverse the lower court's decision against the defendant is made in writing.

As shown in Figure II–1, a criminal case originally tried in a county court may be appealed to a higher state court. Should an appeal fail there, then the defense attorney may carry the appeal to the state supreme court. Since this is the highest court of appeal in a state (except in New York), the court's decision is usually final.

However, there is an exception to this rule. Should the defendant's case involve a question of constitutionality under the

United States Consitution, then an appeal may be made to the United States Supreme Court. This is done by filing for a writ of certiorari with the Supreme Court. If the Court decides there is sufficient reason to review the case then it will obtain all the documents and records relating to the case for review. (For further discussion, see the section on the U.S. Supreme Court under Federal Courts.)

PAROLE

Should the defendant's appeal attempts fail and his conviction be upheld by the various appellate courts, then he will begin serving his sentence. However, it may not be necessary for the accused to serve all of his sentence in prison. Parole is a process whereby the accused, after serving a specified minimum term, may apply for probationary release. Each state has a parole board (as does the federal prison system) that reviews all applications for parole.

The minimum term to be served varies not only with the crime committed, but also from state to state. As previously pointed out in the discussion of sentencing, some offenses result in a minimum–maximum sentence. The minimum term specified in such cases is the time that must be served in prison before parole can be considered. For example, in a "3 to 7 year" sentence, at least 3 years must be spent in prison before parole is possible. In some states, when a minimum–maximum sentence is not required, at least one-third of the sentence must be served prior to application for parole. Other states set a statutory minimum requirement of a specific number of years depending on the offense.

A release on parole is similar to a release on probation in that the defendant remains under the court system's supervision. The term of parole often is for the duration of the defendant's sentence. So long as the defendant remains on "good behavior," commits no further criminal offenses and meets the other requirements of his parole, he may remain out of prison. Violation of parole can, of course, result in his return to prison to serve the remaining sentence in prison.

COMMUTATION

Another possible avenue of leniency toward a convicted person is the commutation of his sentence. This is what is referred to as "an executive action'" that results in the reduction of the term to be served. The action may be taken only by the governor of a state for state offenses or by the President of the United States for federal offenses. Normally, such an action would be taken if the governor or president felt that the sentence imposed was too severe for the offense committed and for the circumstances surrounding the case.

PARDON

The final post-sentencing procedure to consider is the pardon. This action, again invoked by either a governor for state offenses or by the President of the United States for federal offenses, permanently frees the convicted person from his sentence. Perhaps the most famous modern-day example of a presidential pardon is the pardoning of former President Nixon by President Ford. Additionally, the effect of the pardon is to also remove the conviction from the person's record. For example, in some states a convicted felon may not serve on a jury. The pardon allows jury duty service as it, in effect, clears the defendant's record of the conviction (and assuming there are no other previous convictions which the pardon would have no effect on).

Chapter 9

JUVENILE CRIMINAL COURT PROCEDURES

There are several aspects of a juvenile's conduct in relation to the martial arts which could result in his being arrested as a juvenile delinquent:

1. Committing a crime.
2. Violating any state or federal law or city ordinance.
3. Disorderly conduct.
4. Causing injury to another person.

However, a juvenile below a certain age (which varies from state to state) cannot be arrested for a crime and tried in an adult criminal court. Below a specified age in each state, juvenile courts have jurisdiction over youth offenders; whereas over a specified age adult criminal courts have jurisdiction (see Figure I–1 for a listing of these ages by state). Thus the American criminal court system actually has two divisions–juvenile courts and adult courts. The benefit of conviction in a juvenile court is that the youth does not acquire a criminal record.

ARREST

The first step in juvenile court procedures is the arrest of the youth. An officer can arrest any youth who he believes either is in the process of committing an offense or has committed an offense. "Offense" in this sense refers to any illegal act including causing unjustified injury to another person.

As an example, suppose Officer Brown sees a 15-year-old using nunchakus to severely beat another youth. Use of these weapons is illegal in several cities and Officer Brown, being in one of these cities, arrests the youth. If the youth were an adult and had attacked the other person without justification, he can be charged in a criminal court with both battery and assault with a deadly weapon. As a youth, however, he can only be charged with juvenile delinquency.

As another example, 14-year-old George "gets even" with another youth for "stealing his girlfriend" by starting a fight. During the fight, George kicks the other youth in the mouth knocking out his front teeth. The youth's parents file charges against George with the police. George can be arrested for juvenile delinquency but cannot be charged with having committed battery because battery is a crime and George is under age to be charged in an adult criminal court. Therefore he would be brought into juvenile court.

POST ARREST

Once arrested, the police have several options as to how the case may be handled:

1. If the offense is of a nonserious nature, the youth may be merely reprimanded and released with no report being filed against the youth.
2. If the offense is slightly more serious but the youth has no history of trouble, the youth can be given a stern lecture and released with a formal report entered into the juvenile files.
3. If the offense is serious, the case can be directly referred to the juvenile court. The youth can be released to his pa-

rents or gaurdian by providing a written guarantee that he will appear in court.

4. If the youth is considered dangerous or likely to escape, he can be held in custody by the court.

CONSTITUTIONAL RIGHTS

In 1966 the Constitutional rights of juveniles were greatly clarified and enhanced by a United States Supreme Court decision in the Gault case. (Gault was a 15-year-old youth who was given a possible 6-year correctional institution sentence for making an obscene phone call. The adult penalty for the same offense was a fine of $5 to $50 or a maximum 2-month jail sentence.) As a result of this now famous Court decision, certain guarantees must be met by police and courts when dealing with juveniles:

1. The charge(s) against the juvenile must be presented in writing both to him and to his parents or guardian.
2. The juvenile must be informed of his right to have a lawyer represent him.
3. Upon questioning and interrogation, the juvenile must be informed of his right to remain silent if he so chooses.
4. The juvenile and his lawyer have the right to confront and cross-examine any witnesses who testify against the youth.
5. The juvenile must be found guilty beyond a reasonable doubt in order to be convicted of juvenile delinquency.
6. The juvenile is not to be tried in front of a jury; instead the juvenile court judge decides the verdict after hearing all witnesses and studying all evidence relating to the case.

PETITION

After being arrested, if the youth is not released from the court's jurisdiction due to the seriousness of his offense, then a petition identifying the youth and stating his offense is filed with the juvenile court. (In adult courts the petition would be either an indictment or a complaint.)

HEARING

The juvenile court judge will then hold a hearing to inform both the youth and his parents or guardian of the charges against him. Juvenile hearings are informal as compared to adult court proceedings. Since there is no trial by jury, the hearing is held in the judge's chambers. Neither the public nor any press reporter are allowed to attend. The press is not allowed to publish the juvenile's name. Upon receiving a petition, the juvenile court will assign a probation officer to investigate both the case and the youth's background. The probation officer's report and recommendations have a strong influence on the judge's verdict. During the probation officer's investigation, the youth will be released to his parents or guardian unless he is considered as either dangerous or likely to escape.

VERDICT

The judge's verdict can take one of several forms:

1. Dismissing the case without convicting the youth, due to either insufficient evidence or clear lack of guilt on the juvenile's part.
2. Placing the juvenile on probation with release to his parents or guardian.
3. Sentencing to a training center or correctional institution (reformatory) or detention in a youth home.
4. In addition to numbers two and three above, the judge may also order payment (restitution) for any physical damage or injury inflicted by the juvenile.

As with adult convictions, a juvenile conviction can be appealed and reviewed in a separate hearing.

Part III

CIVIL LAW PROCEDURE

Chapter 10

CIVIL LAW AND COURT PROCEDURE

TORT LAW DEFINITION

The second important division of law concerning the martial arts is tort, or civil, law. Whereas crime deals with the relationships of citizens and governments, torts deal with the relationships of citizens with citizens. The following sections will provide a more detailed definition of the subject of tort law. Additionally, the types of torts that martial arts students might become involved with are discussed. Finally, the topic of liability is examined. The final section of the chapter deals with civil court procedures; that is, what to expect should you become involved in a civil lawsuit.

GENERAL

A tort is a civil wrong. Tort law controls the relationships of citizens with each other. It allows a citizen who has been intentionally, or negligently, harmed by another citizen to seek justice under the law. The usual punishment for a person found guilty of unjustly harming another person is to require the guilty person to pay monetary compensation to the injured person. This is referred to as "damages." Thus tort law provides for the payment of monetary damages by one person to another; whereas, criminal law requires either payment of fines by a person to the state and/or imprisonment of the guilty person.

The basic requirements that must be met before the court will consider that a tort has been committed are; a person must have been wrongfully harmed, by another person, either intentionally or negligently. "Wrongfully harmed" means that some specific law has been violated by the offending person. However, it will have to be determined by the jury whether the wrongful harm was done intentionally, accidentally, or negligently. Additionally, it is inherent in this definition that some damage occurred as a result of the wrongful harm. There can be no tort offense present unless damage has resulted from an illegal act.

INTENT, ACCIDENT, AND NEGLIGENCE

Intent is a condition of the mind whereby a person wishes to perform a certain act. Accident is a situation in which a person acts as carefully as could be reasonably expected of any average person, yet an undesired result occurs anyway. Negligence occurs when a person does not wish a certain situation to occur, but because the person is so careless and thoughtless about his actions, the unfortunate results take place anyway.

It is obvious, then, that there is no intent or wishful state of mind in either accident or negligence. Further, in accident, the person has acted with due care and reasonableness. Accident is normally a legal defense against an accusation of having committed a tort. On the other hand, intent and negligence are the two primary actions leading to commission of a tort.

CIVIL COURT PROCEDURE

In this chapter we will discuss the procedural steps that are followed in civil lawsuits. The procedures in criminal court cases were earlier examined. There are differences between the two types of court actions as will be seen in the discussion. The bulk of the section will be concerned with the procedures preliminary to a trial, the trial, and the actions that may occur subsequent to a trial.

PROCEDURAL REQUIREMENTS

Before a civil lawsuit can be initiated, there are several requirements that must be first satisfied. These include the statute of limitations and the jurisdiction of the court.

Statute of Limitations

A statute of limitations defines the time period during which a civil lawsuit may be brought against a tort offender. If you or your property have been injured because of a tort committed by a person, and you do not sue the person within the statutory time limit, then you have no legal recourse to recover damages from that person. The time limit begins with the date on which the tort was committed. These statutes vary according to both the state and the tort. These are not federal statutes and are set, therefore, by each state as it deems proper. As shown in Figure III–1, the limitation for suit for personal injury varies from one to six years, for wrongful death from one to six years, for assault and battery from one to six years, and trespass or conversion from two to six years.

Jurisdiction

It is most important that a civil lawsuit be initiated in the correct court of jurisdiction. Of course, a private citizen generally has no knowledge as to which court is the correct one. This is one of the important reasons for seeking out a competent attorney when contemplating a civil legal action. Should a civil case be brought before a court not having jurisdiction over the matter,

FIGURE III–1

Time Limit for Initiating a Civil Lawsuit in Years

State	**Damage to Personal Property**	**Assault and/or Battery**	**Personal Injury**	**Wrongful Death**
Alabama	6	1	1	2
Alaska	6	2	2	2
Arizona	2	2	2	2
Arkansas	3	1	3	3
California	3	1	1	1
Colorado	6	1	1	2
Connecticut	2	2	2	2
Delaware	2	2	2	2
District of Columbia	3	1	1	1
Florida	3	2	4	2
Georgia	4	2	3	2
Hawaii	2	2	2	2
Idaho	3	2	2	2
Illinois	5	2	2	2
Indiana	2	2	2	2
Iowa	5	2	2	2
Kansas	2	1	2	2
Kentucky	5	1	1	1
Louisiana	1	1	1	1
Maine	6	2	6	2
Maryland	3	1	3	2
Massachusetts	2	2	2	2
Michigan	3	2	3	3
Minnesota	6	2	2	3
Mississippi	6	1	6	6
Missouri	5	2	5	1
Montana	2	2	2	3
Nebraska	4	1	4	2
Nevada	3	2	2	2
New Hampshire	6	2	2	2
New Jersey	6	2	2	2
New Mexico	4	3	3	3
New York	3	1	3	2
North Carolina	3	1	3	2
North Dakota	6	2	6	2
Ohio	2	1	2	2

FIGURE III–1 Cont'd

Time Limit for Initiating a Civil Lawsuit in Years

State	**Damage to Personal Property**	**Assault and/or Battery**	**Personal Injury**	**Wrongful Death**
Oklahoma	2	1	2	2
Oregon	6	2	2	3
Pennsylvania	6	2	2	1
Rhode Island	6	6	2	2
South Carolina	6	2	6	6
South Dakota	6	2	3	3
Tennessee	3	1	1	1
Texas	2	2	2	2
Utah	3	1	4	2
Vermont	3	3	3	2
Virginia	5	2	2	2
Washington	3	2	3	3
West Virginia	2	2	2	2
Wisconsin	6	2	3	3
Wyoming	4	1	4	2

the defending attorney can request dismissal of the case. Sometimes it may even be possible that such a dismissal may prevent the suit from being brought before any other court.

PRELIMINARY REQUIREMENTS

Prior to any civil trial, there are several preliminary procedural steps which must be taken. First, a complaint must be filed by the injured person against the wrong doer. Second, the court must issue a summons to bring the defendant into court. Third, the defendant may file an answer to the charge against him. (See Figure III–2.)

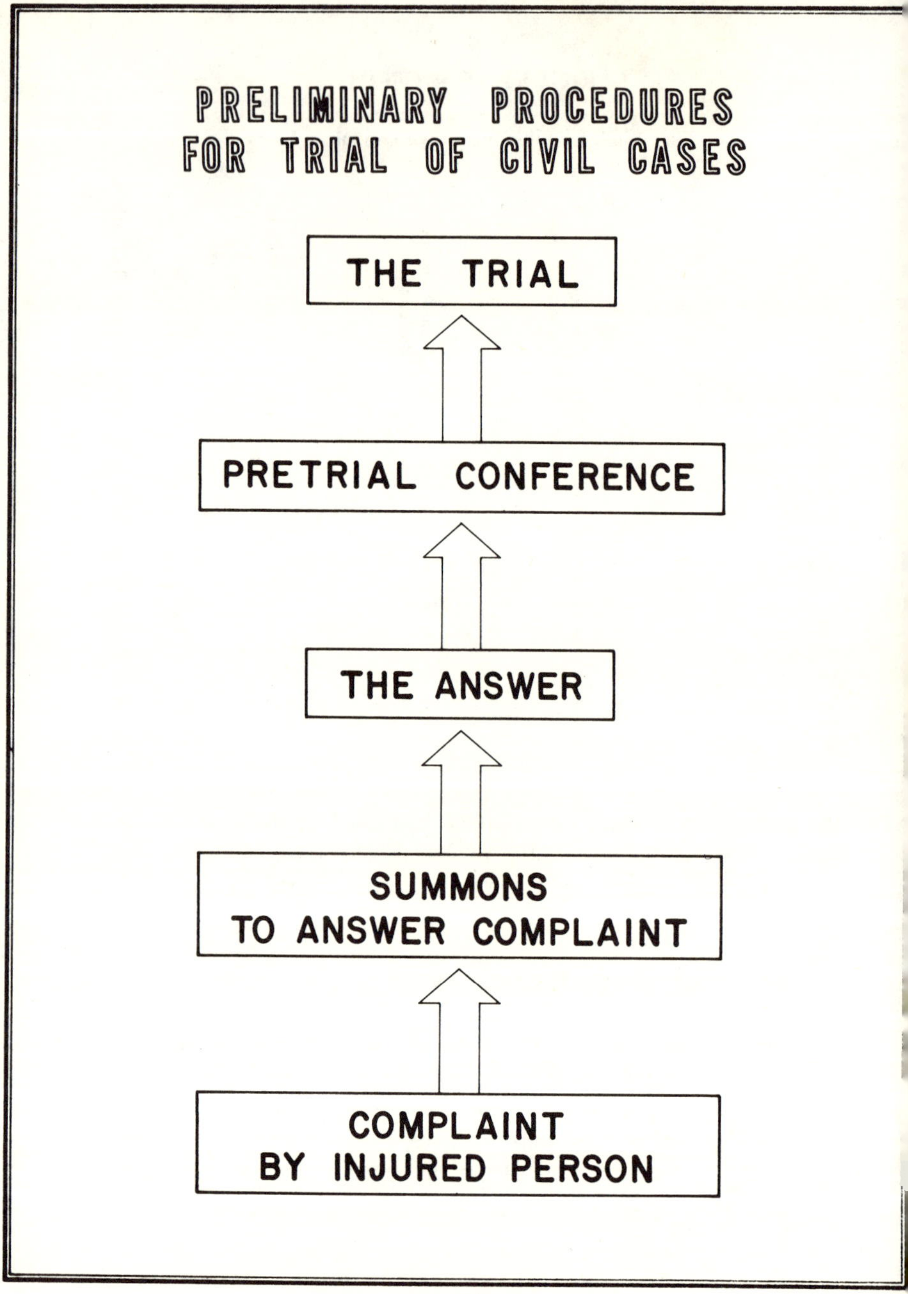
PRELIMINARY PROCEDURES
FOR TRIAL OF CIVIL CASES
THE TRIAL
PRETRIAL CONFERENCE
THE ANSWER
SUMMONS
TO ANSWER COMPLAINT
COMPLAINT
BY INJURED PERSON

FIGURE III–2

Complaint

The initiation of any civil action against a person begins with the filing of a complaint by the injured person. The complaint is a written document stating the charge (the complaint), the person causing the injury, and what compensation the injured person is seeking. Particularly, the complaint must contain all of the facts associated with the reason for which the plaintiff is suing the defendant. For example, if you sue me for damages caused when I struck you in the mouth causing you to lose two front teeth, these facts must be stated in the complaint.

The reasoning behind the requirement for the specific facts of the complaint is to give the defendant specific notice of what charge he must defend himself against in court. In civil cases, the complaint is the initial action taken by an injured party (the plaintiff) against the person causing the damage (the defendant). However, the complaint itself does not prove anything. Through the complaint, the plaintiff alleges that the defendant was the cause of certain damage or injury to the plaintiff. The court process will determine the guilt or innocence of the defendant. The statement of the facts can be very brief as full development of them will occur in court.

Summons

Once the plaintiff files his complaint with the court, the defendant is notified of the plaintiff's having initiated civil suit against him. The court notifies the defendant of the suit by issuing a summons. This is a court order which demands that the defendant answer the complaint against him. An authorized court official (police officer, sheriff's deputy, process-server) delivers the summons personally to the defendant. The summons states the nature of the complaint, the court having jurisdiction over the suit, and requires that an answer be made by the defendant to the complaint. Of particular importance is the time limit specified in the summons within which the answer must be made. Should the defendant fail to answer the summons within the time limit, the court will render a judgment allowing the plaintiff to win his case by default.

It should be noted that a summons can only be served within the jurisdictional area of the court handling the suit. If the defendant lives outside of this area, the court must wait until the defendant enters the area before serving him with the summons. Thus if you intend to bring a civil suit against a person, make certain that the court issuing the summons will have access to serve him the summons. For suits where the plaintiff and the defendant are geographically widely separated, it is possible for the plaintiff to file his complaint in a court having jurisdiction over the defendant's residence, but not over the plaintiff's residence just to facilitate the serving of the summons.

For example, if I live in X county and you live in Y county, I can file the complaint in your Y county. However, if you work at an office in my X county, then the complaint can be filed in X county and you will be served the summons at your office.

Answer

The initial answer to the plaintiff's complaint may take several forms:

1. If the complaint is unclear to the defendant, he and his attorney may request a more detailed statement of facts (referred to as a bill of particulars). Subsequent to receiving this data, the defendant and his attorney can then file their written answer.
2. The defendant's attorney either initially or subsequent to receiving the bill of particulars, may ask for a summary judgment. This is a request that the court dismiss the case on the basis of insufficient evidence against the defendant.
3. The defendant's attorney may initially respond to the summons by filing a demurrer. This is a request that the court dismiss the case on the basis of the plaintiff being

incorrect in filing the complaint. The request does not necessarily deny the truth of the plaintiff's complaint; rather, it attacks some other aspect of the suit. For example, the suit may have been filed in the wrong court of jurisdiction, or the statute of limitations may have expired.

4. The defendant's attorney may file his written answer denying the facts of the complaint. Or he may admit the facts but deny the plaintiff's interpretation of them. For example, the plaintiff may claim that the defendant struck him in the mouth causing the loss of two teeth and that the action constituted battery. The defendant, on the other hand, may view the action as having been self-defense. It will be up to the court (and the jury) to decide which interpretation is correct.

Subsequent to the filing of the defendant's answer, the plaintiff's attorney is allowed to file a reply. This is merely the comments of the plaintiff's attorney on the defendant's answer—usually refuting whatever is said in the answer.

Pre-trial Conference

As discussed under criminal court procedures, the American system of justice involves a great deal of bargaining. Such bargaining in criminal cases is between the prosecutor (often the district attorney) and the defendant's attorney. If the defendant is clearly guilty with no hope of acquittal by a jury, this system of bargaining will often produce a less severe sentence for the defendant than if he were to plead innocent, go through a jury trial, and be found guilty. The bargaining is done simply to reduce the workload on the court system.

Likewise, in the civil court system, a similar bargaining process takes place. In these cases, however, the bargaining is between the defendant's attorney and the plaintiff's attorney. For example, in the case where I knocked your two teeth out, let us suppose that the evidence clearly rules out self-defense and strongly suggests that I committed battery. My attorney, rather than risk a guilty finding by the jury together with a penalty of substantial financial damages, will attempt to settle out of court for an amount sufficient to pay your medical expenses and legal fees. If this is all you wanted anyway, then you'll be satisfied. Additionally, although I'll have to pay, I should be happy to not have the additional costs of a court trial (which I would pay if found guilty) and possibly higher damages (such as punitive damages if it was shown that I wantonly and deliberately knocked your teeth out with my martial arts kick or punch).

There is nothing illegal or "shady" about such bargaining. It works to the benefit of the plaintiff, the defendant, and the court system. The civil pre-trial conference is conducted with the judge present who acts more as a mediator between the two sides in an effort to develop an equitable solution to the suit.

TRIAL

This section will discuss the procedures of a civil trial. Included will be jury selection, trial procedures, and the types of damages a jury may award. The trial procedures will differ in some respects from those of a criminal trial. (See Figure III–3.)

The awarding of damages by a jury to an injured party in a civil suit is of particular significance to the martial arts student. This is the point at which misuse of your techniques can become quite expensive. Such awards can total thousands of dollars and you must pay! A later section will discuss the means through which the court may enforce collection from you.

The Jury

The jury selection was previously described for criminal trials and is identical for civil trials. In fact, in many jurisdictions, when a person is selected to serve on petit jury duty for a period of time (two weeks, for example), he may serve on both civil case

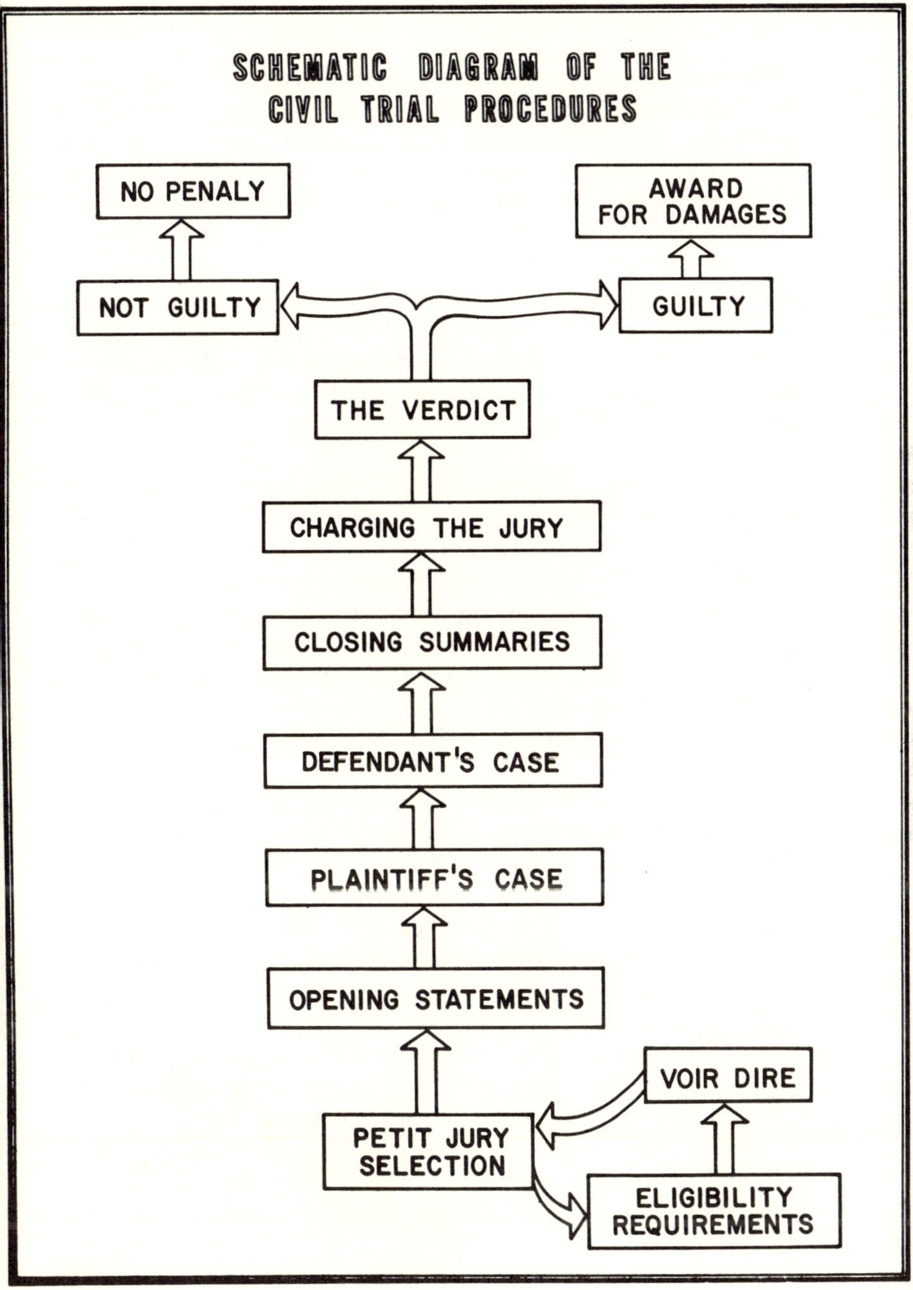
SCHEMATIC DIAGRAM OF THE CIVIL TRIAL PROCEDURES
NO PENALY
AWARD FOR DAMAGES
NOT GUILTY
GUILTY
THE VERDICT
CHARGING THE JURY
CLOSING SUMMARIES
DEFENDANT'S CASE
PLAINTIFF'S CASE
OPENING STATEMENTS
VOIR DIRE
PETIT JURY SELECTION
ELIGIBILITY REQUIREMENTS

FIGURE III–3

juries and minor criminal case juries. (Such cases may take only a day or two for trial, thus during two weeks, a member of the jury panel may have a chance to serve on more than one case as a juror.) As described for criminal cases, the defending and complaining attorneys have the right of peremptory challenges and challenges for cause in order to select those jury members having no biases against any aspect of the civil case. (Remember that this process of jury selection is called the voir dire.) As in criminal cases, the primary function of the jury is to determine what the facts of the case are based on the presentations by the attorneys in the case. The function of the judge is to interpret the law as it applies to the civil case.

Civil Trial Procedures

As in criminal trials, in a civil trial the attorneys initially present their case to the jury in a brief format called the opening statement. The object of this opening synopsis of the case is to inform the jury what the case is about and what each side of the case intends to attempt to prove to the jury. As in a criminal trial, the plaintiff's attorney is allowed to make the first opening statement.

Also the plaintiff is allowed to present his case first. His lawyer may present whatever evidence and witnesses he finds necessary in order to best prove his case. Similar to criminal cases, expert witnesses may be presented for specialized fields relating to the case. Also the defending attorney is permitted to cross-examine any of the plaintiff's witnesses.

Subsequent to presentation of the plaintiff's case, the defense is allowed to present its side of the case. Likewise, the defending attorney may present any evidence or witnesses he deems necessary to support his client's side of the case. Plaintiff's attorney has the right to cross-examine any defense witnesses.

Subsequent to the presentation of their cases by the plaintiff's and defendant's attorneys, the attorneys make their closing summaries. As with the opening statements, the closing summaries are made for the benefit of the jury. Each attorney outlines what he believes that he has proved in his case.

The judge then "charges the jury." That is, he interprets the law for the jury as it applies to the case. He informs the jury as to what questions they must answer in order to rule for one side or the other. In criminal cases, we discussed that the defendant could be found guilty only if the prosecutor had proved beyond a reasonable doubt that the defendant was, in fact, guilty. However, in a civil case, the requirement for determining guilt is not quite so demanding on the jury. The plaintiff need only demonstrate that the "preponderance of evidence" indicates the defendant's guilt. Thus if the jury finds that the evidence predominantly supports the plaintiff's claim of injury caused by the defendant, then the jury must return a verdict of guilty against the defendant.

Jury Awarded Damages

Probably the most significant aspect of the entire discussion of civil court procedures, as it relates to the martial arts, is the awarding of damages by the jury. Damages, in this sense, means financial reimbursement that must be paid by the defendant to the plaintiff. The only method by which a civil law court can force a defendant to make restitution for any damage (destruction, physical harm, loss of property, loss of income) he caused the plaintiff by committing a wrongful act (violated the law) is payment of money. If necessary, the court will authorize the sheriff to sell defendant's property and forward the cash proceeds to the plaintiff in order to fulfill the court's judgment.

Thus of significance to the martial arts is the fact that if you injure a person through the illegal misuse of your techniques, the injured person may not only file criminal charges against you, he may also seek damages from you in a civil law court. There are three types of damages which the jury may award, i.e. nominal damages, punitive or exemplary damages, and compensatory damages. (See Figure III–4.)

TYPES OF CIVIL DAMAGES

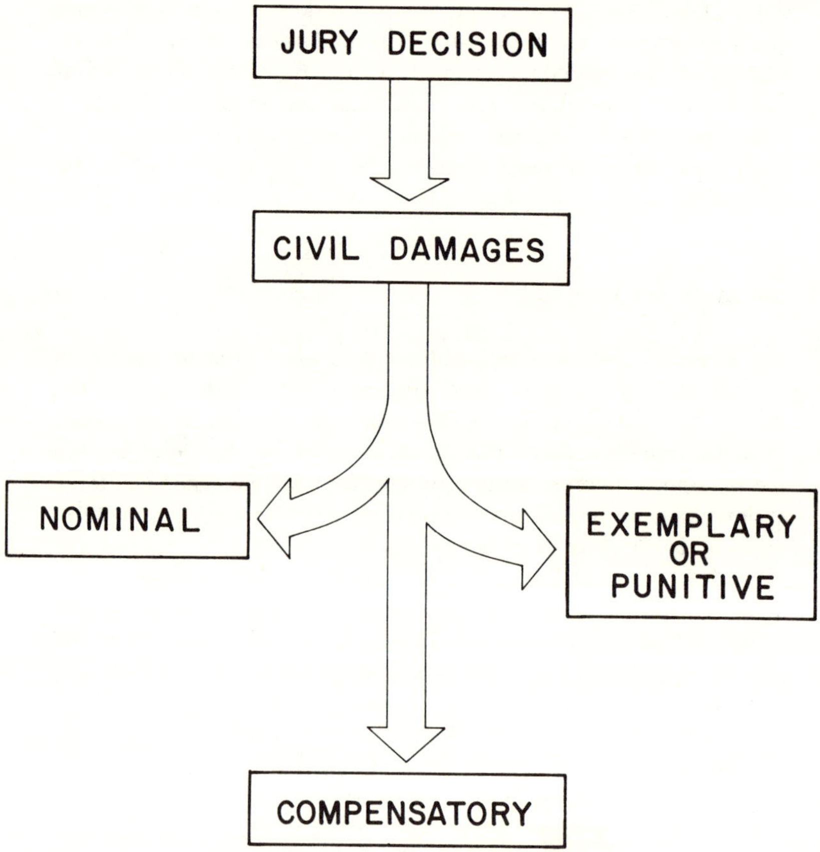

FIGURE III–4

In order for a jury to award damages, two basic requirements must both be met in the case. First, the defendant must have violated a law. Second, the defendant must have caused damage to the plaintiff through the act that violated the law. Because of these two requirements, it is not possible for an attacker who is injured by your self-defense techniques to recover damages from you in court. The reason is that self-defense is legal. A person who illegally attacks another person forfeits his legal rights to recover damages in a civil court should his victim cause injury to the attacker. However, if the defender goes beyond reasonableness and prudence in his defense, then the attacker may sue for damages. For example, if a slightly drunk man attempts to punch you without cause and you knock him down and then brutally kick him repeatedly once he is down, you have gone beyond reasonable bounds in your defense. The drunk may sue you to recover damages for his injuries caused by your excessive beating.

Nominal Damages

Nominal damages are awarded when a plaintiff's rights have been violated, however, the plaintiff suffered no damage from the illegal act. To sue for nominal damages would be to merely establish that the plaintiff did, in fact, have a right which was violated by the defendant. A common award in such cases is $1.00. Nominal damages are classified as noncompensatory damages because no damage resulted to the plaintiff from the defendant's act. As will be discussed in more detail later, compensatory damages can be recovered only if the defendant's act causes damage or harm to the plaintiff.

Suppose, as an example, that I commit assault against you. If you recall, the definition of assault states that it is a threat to injure, which appears believable to the plaintiff. No physical contact is necessary in assault. However, committing assault violates a person's right to personal safety as well as the law. In the example, my committing assault against you was a wrongful and illegal act but it caused no damage or harm to you. Consequently, only nominal damages may be sued for in civil court. (Of course, you may also file a charge of assault against me in criminal court.)

Exemplary Damages

Exemplary damages are a punitive judgment against the defendant. A jury may award exemplary damages in cases where the defendant is proved to have acted in a brutal manner toward the plaintiff with complete disregard for the plaintiff's health and physical well-being. These are referred to as punitive damages because the jury intends them to serve as a punishment for the defendant. They are referred to as exemplary damages because the jury intends them to be an example to anyone else contemplating a similar illegal act.

There is no standard award for any given case which the jury must follow. Rather, every jury may award exemplary damages in the amount it deems justifiable for the case. The only restriction is that the award must be reasonable and not excessive. If the award is excessive in the court's opinion, the court may either reduce the award or nullify it. Consider an example where a beggar pleads with you for money. You refuse to give him anything and he becomes enraged. Because he attempts to strike you, you defend yourself and punch him in the solar plexus whereupon he falls down. Your aversion to beggars makes you decide to teach him a lesson, whereupon you viciously and repeatedly kick his ribs while he is down. In such a case, the jury would be allowed to return a judgement against you for punitive damages.

Compensatory Damages

Compensatory damages are awarded by a jury for that damage or harm to a person measurable in financial terms. It is the plaintiff's obligation in such a case to present to the jury adequate data and evidence to allow them to determine the amount of damages to award. For example, such data might include doctor and hospital bills in the event of physical injury to the plaintiff. Additionally, if plaintiff owned his own small one-man business, his stay in a hospital, if lengthy, could adversely affect his income. If his business were steady and had produced a rather constant level of income for several years, the jury could utilize such data in order to award compensatory damages for loss of income to the plaintiff.

It is important to note that financially measureable harm must be suffered by the plaintiff as a result of the defendant's illegal and wrongful act in order for a jury to award compensatory damages. Further, the jury's award will be for all damage resulting from the defendant's act. Thus if plaintiff had medical expenses and loss of income, the jury's award would take all of these into consideration. The significance is that if you illegally injure someone with your martial art techniques, then he must attempt to collect all damages, for all his expenses and losses resulting from your act, from you in a single suit.

Another important point is that the jury may also award compensatory damages for any future loss or expense the plaintiff may suffer as a result of the defendant's wrongful act. For example, suppose that you wrongfully damage a person's nervous system with a strong punch or kick to the person's head. If expert medical testimony by physicians demonstrates a reasonable probability that the person will have recurring physical problems as a result of your illegal act, the jury will take this into consideration when totalling the person's losses to determine the damages to award.

As another example, suppose that you punch a person very strongly in the head and knock him unconscious. He falls to the ground striking his head on the concrete sidewalk. A few weeks after his apparent recovery, he sues you in civil court and recovers compensatory damages for his medical expenses. Several months later he begins to suffer periods of dizziness. A few days after the dizziness begins his left side becomes paralyzed. Medical tests strongly indicate that the dizziness and paralysis have resulted from the injury caused by you several months earlier and plaintiff has not injured himself in any manner since then. If the person again sues you in a civil court to recover compensatory damages for the expense of his paralysis, he will not be allowed to recover since he has already sued you for the illegal act. The plaintiff can only sue the defendant once for a wrongful act causing harm or damage. If any future injuries or loss will likely occur to the plaintiff because of defendant's act, then this must be clearly demonstrated to the jury during the trial. The jury will then take this into consideration when determining the amount of damages to award.

Compensatory damages can be awarded for mental suffering (even though it is not measurable in financial terms) provided that the mental suffering is a direct result of physical damage or injuries caused by the defendant's illegal act. For instance, suppose you wrongfully use your martial arts techniques and kick a person in the spine thereby breaking his back. As a result, he is permanently crippled. In a civil suit, the jury can take into account the mental grief associated with being permanently crippled as well as all financially measurable expenses associated with the injury.

If you deliberately and intentionally frighten a person through assault, he may sue you in civil court. Mental anguish caused by a deliberate, wrongful and illegal act can result in compensatory damages being awarded even though no physical injury resulted from the act. However, as a realistic consideration, such fright may be difficult to prove to a jury. Obtaining an award in such a case will not be easy.

Now consider what will happen if the plaintiff dies as a result of injuries caused by the defendant, but his death is subsequent to having sued the defendant. Under the laws of the majority of states, the defendant is still obligated to pay the awarded damages to the plaintiff's estate (which, in effect, means the plaintiff's family). In legal terminology, it is said that the obligation of the defendant to pay damages does not die with the plaintiff.

In some states, if the plaintiff had not sued the defendant before his death, the plaintiff's estate (family) would have the right to sue just as if the plaintiff had lived to do so. Thus the law does not allow the right to take civil action against a defendant to die with the plaintiff. The right is said to "survive" the plaintiff.

POST-TRIAL ACTIONS

Once the trial has concluded, the jury passes its verdict, and the judge renders final judgment against the defendant (assuming that the jury finds the defendant guilty and awards damages), there are several further legal actions that may occur.

First, the defendant may not accept the court's verdict. He has the right, through his attorney, to appeal the case to a higher court for review. In all likelihood, the civil case originated in a county court and the verdict was passed by a petit jury. At the time the judge renders judgment against the defendant, the defendant's attorney informs the court of the intent to appeal. There is a time limitation within which the actual appeal must be filed with the proper court of jurisdiction.

Second, and quite simply, the defendant may accept the court's judgment against him. As a result, he pays to the plaintiff all damages awarded by the court.

Third, and somewhat involved, the defendant may arbitrarily decide not to pay anything to the plaintiff. In such an instance, the plaintiff can request that the court enforce its judgment against the defendant. The court has the power to authorize an officer of the court (frequently the sheriff) to take one of several actions against the defendant in order to enforce payment of the damages:

1. Attachment. The sheriff can take possession of a sufficient amount of the defendant's property, which, when sold at a public sheriff's auction, will provide adequate money to satisfy the damages award.
2. Garnishment. The defendant's employer can be required to withhold a portion of the defendant's wages, forward

the amount to the court, which in turn will pay the plaintiff. The garnishment procedure will continue until the plaintiff's award has been paid.

3. Arrest. The sheriff can be ordered to arrest the defendant and bring him before the court. After hearing the defendant's explanation as to why payment has been delayed, if the court is not satisfied, the defendant can be jailed until the damages award is paid to the plaintiff.

Part IV

LEGAL IMPLICATIONS FOR THE SCHOOL AND INSTRUCTOR

Chapter 11

LEGAL IMPLICATIONS FOR THE SCHOOL AND INSTRUCTOR

It is appropriate in connection with discussing the legal implications of self-defense to also discuss the legal implications for the martial arts school and the martial arts instructor. The major points to be covered include adequate supervision during classes, injuries to students during class or tournaments, and injuries to spectators during class or tournaments. Finally, a suggested liability release form is presented.

This entire chapter is concerned with the subject of tort law and not with criminal law. As discussed in earlier chapters, tort law deals with the violation of the rights of an individual by another individual. Previous chapters on civil law were designed for the student of self-defense and the possible result should he misuse his techniques. In this chapter, the discussion is intended for the martial arts instructor.

INTENT, NEGLIGENCE, ACCIDENT

Within the field of tort or civil law, we will concentrate the discussion on *negligence*. It is important to note the distinction between negligence, intention, and accident. *Intent* means that you want a certain outcome to occur, and therefore is a state of mind. *Negligence* means that you do not want a certain outcome to occur, but you are not careful enough to prevent the outcome. *Accident* means that you do not want a certain outcome to occur and even though you exert a reasonable amount of care, the outcome occurs anyway.

As a martial arts instructor, consider that you deliberately kick a student in the rib cage very hard thereby fracturing several of his ribs. This is intent on your part. Suppose you use a spinning back round kick and deliberately strike a student in the head causing a serious brain concussion. This is intent because you wanted to strike the student in the head with strong force.

On the other hand, suppose you kick at a student's side with force, not intending to hit him during a demonstration of the kick, but you fracture his ribs. At the time, the student is standing still as a target for your demonstration not expecting to be kicked. A similar example is when you kick the target student in the head with a spinning back round kick during a demonstration. In both instances, the intent on your part was absent. However, it could be argued in a court of law that you, as an instructor and student of advanced rank, should have enough control to avoid hitting a student standing still. Negligence could be claimed against you in both cases.

As an example of accident suppose you and a student of rank equal to yours are free sparring in a tournament. During the contest, you punch your opponent in the nose causing severe bleeding requiring medical attention. You did not desire to injure your opponent and were not trying to actually strike him. Unfortunately, he moved forward just as you punched. Since you used as much care as could be expected during the contest and did not desire to injure the opponent, this would be an accident.

NEGLIGENCE

Three elements must be present in order for an instructor to be found liable for injury resulting from negligence:

1. Legal obligation to use care in regard to others (students and spectators).
2. Failure to use care.
3. Injury resulting from the failure to use care.

As the discussion of negligence proceeds, the examples presented will aid in making clear what is meant by "legal obligation" to use care. In regard to using care, a jury or a law court will apply the standard of asking what would the average person do under similar conditions? Thus it is seen that the circumstances will determine the amount of care to be used in a given situation. In addition, it can be said that the ability of the instructor, both to teach and to physically perform, will be part of the circumstances that a court might take into account in a negligence suit.

The final and third element necessary is that actual injury must occur in order for a negligence suit to be brought into court. Even though an instructor acts with all-too-apparent negligence, if no one is injured, then the instructor cannot be held liable for negligence. As an example, suppose an instructor takes a group of beginning students into a room, turns out the lights, and tells them to begin practice fighting. If, by some remote chance no injuries occur, then the instructor who obviously acted with negligence escapes liability. If, as most probably would happen, injuries do occur, then the instructor can be held liable for negligence. In fact, he could be sued separately by each injured student. (Although this seems like an absurd example, the author knows of an instance where the instructor did such a thing and with a large group of students! Although injuries did occur, the instructor remarkably escaped any liability suits.)

SUPERVISION

The topic of supervision is most important to the subject of negligence because an instructor's time is predominantly spent supervising classes. Within this supervisory time there are a number of potential sources for negligent injuries to occur for which the instructor could be held liable in a civil court suit. The following discussion will describe these potential negligent situations and will suggest how the instructor may avoid such problems.

HEAD INSTRUCTOR'S COMPETENCY

The obvious point to begin the discussion of supervisory negligence is with the head instructor of the school. Should any injury occur to students or spectators in a school resulting in a lawsuit against the instructor, the instructor's background and competency to operate a school will likely be questioned by the court. It is unfortunate that the martial arts are subject to certain fast buck operators who open a school just long enough to accumulate some cash and then take off leaving disenchanted students behind. Frequently these individuals have little, if any, qualifications to be teaching. It is in these temporary fly-by-night schools that injuries are most likely to occur as the instructor has no concern for the student's safety and well-being.

Fortunately, the majority of instructors are sincere and qualified to teach. As a minimum, it is suggested that a head instructor of a school should be of first degree black belt rank from a recognized martial arts organization of which there are a number in the United States.

A second requirement for the chief instructor is that he have several years of teaching experience directly assisting his instructor. (In the martial arts, black belts often train with a high ranking instructor and then open their own school either as a branch for the high ranking instructor or as their own enterprise.) The previous experience factor is most important. There are a number of situations which arise in martial arts instruction which the high ranking instructor can help his assistant instructors avoid or manage in a competent manner. The martial arts student inexperienced in teaching who sets out to run his own school without guidance may well allow negligent injuries to occur simply from lack of knowledge.

Thus a certificate of rank from a recognized organization and a background of teaching experience are a minimum to prove an instructor's competency to a court of law.

LEAVING CLASS UNATTENDED

An instructor should avoid leaving a training class unattended by either himself or a qualified assistant. An injury occurring during an unsupervised class could be grounds for a negligence suit being brought against the instructor. There are several situations that might arise that could lead to a student's injury; whereas, had an instructor been present the situation could have been avoided.

For example, there is a phone call for the instructor. He goes to an office to answer the phone but has no view of the training classroom from the office. During his absence, two younger students begin playing around in a childish manner and one is injured as a result. The parents of the injured student could claim that had the instructor been present, he could have prevented the horseplay thereby avoiding the injury. Whether or not the court agrees with the parents, the instructor will have the legal expenses of defending himself in court even if he is found innocent of the lawsuit.

As a second example, suppose that the instructor decides to take a cigarette break and leaves the classroom for awhile. During his absence, two students become angry at each other and begin a serious fight resulting in a serious injury to one of the students. The injured student, being older than 21 years of age sues the instructor for negligence due to his absence from the classroom. It could be argued in court that had the instructor been present the loss of tempers could have been quickly subdued by the instructor's intervention thus avoiding the resulting injury.

For a third example, consider that the instructor leaves the classroom for a time in order to make a social telephone call to a friend. During his absence, a beginning student having observed several advanced students practice jumping kicks at the training bags, attempts a similar jumping kick. Having never been shown how to perform the kick, he is unsure what to do.

Nevertheless he incorrectly jumps, misses the bag, and lands on his arm thereby breaking it. The student could sue the instructor for negligence due to his unnecessary absence. It could be reasonably argued that, had the instructor remained in the classroom, he could have prevented the beginner from attempting the technique without proper instruction thus avoiding the injury.

DIRECT INJURY TO A STUDENT

Some instructors, probably unknowingly, open themselves to negligence lawsuits by their causing a direct injury to a student. In this type of situation, the instructor attempts to prove his superiority of technique and deliberately injures a student during practice fighting. In a civil court, it would be extremely difficult for an instructor to justify such action on his part. Whether the instructor's purpose was ego-building, image maintenance, saving face, retaliation, etc., is immaterial in the court. An instructor of higher rank than any other member of the class would be presumed to have the utmost control of both his mental and physical self. (Further, an instructor will gain no economic benefit by deliberately injuring a student thereby preventing his training and possibly frightening off other students. Yet the author knows of several instances where instructors have deliberately injured students to prove their ability. They have escaped civil lawsuits probably only because the students were not aware of their legal rights.)

COMPETENCY OF ASSISTANT INSTRUCTORS

Another potential source of negligence action against an instructor is the competency or qualifications of the assistant instructors who teach in the chief instructor's absence. An assistant instructor having very little experience under the chief instructor's guidance may allow some of the situations to occur which this chapter cautions against. Should an injury occur to a student because of the assistant's negligence, either he or the chief instructor or both, may be sued for negligence in allowing the injury to occur.

For example, suppose a visitor to the class wishes to practice with the students. The assistant instructor allows him to do so. However, it is the chief instructor's policy not to allow visitors to practice with classes, but he failed to inform the assistant of this rule. The visitor has poor control and seriously injures a student. It is possible for both the assistant or chief instructors to be sued for negligence.

DISCIPLINE

Many martial arts injuries in class can be prevented by the instructor maintaining strong discipline in class. This discipline includes the instructor himself, the class as a whole, and individuals within the class.

Instructor

It may seem unnecessary to many martial arts instructors to discuss the self-discipline of the instructor (and for many well-qualified instructors it is unnecessary), but his direct physical actions in demonstrating or practicing with students can result in a negligence suit if he directly causes injury to a student. As mentioned earlier, the author knows of instances (and suffered one himself) where an instructor, in order to "save face," will, deliberately injure a student. This is, without a doubt, a display of lack of self-discipline on the instructor's part. In the legal framework of American society, such action on the part of the instructor could be subject to a civil lawsuit. Probably there are not more lawsuits because students are not aware of their legal rights.

Some instructors, particularly the fly-by-nighters who quickly come and go, are rather immature concerning their own self-discipline. The instructor who is periodically absent from class for a cigarette break, who makes social telephone calls during class, who tells students to do a certain technique and leaves the classroom for 30 minutes is demonstrating a lack of self-discipline. His absence from the class leaving it unsupervised can lead to injuries which could have been prevented by his presence. It could be argued in court that his absence from class for an unnecessary reason constitutes negligence. It will require the instructor's time and expense to defend himself against such a suit.

Class Discipline

One of the greatest potential areas in which a negligence suit for injury can occur is failure of the instructor to maintain class discipline. Particularly, preteenage children will indulge in "horseplay" unless firmly kept under control by the instructor. In legal terminology, the instructor is acting in *loco parentis*, which means that he is dealing with the children in place of the parents. He is a substitute parent while the child is in the classroom. Of course teenage and older students may also play around on occasion which could result in injury.

It is obvious then that an instructor should maintain strong class discipline at all times while students are in the changing rooms, on the training floor, and even outside the gym. If it is made quite clear to students that no playing around with techniques will be tolerated, then one possible source of negligence lawsuits will be eliminated.

Corporal Punishment

Corporal punishment means physical contact with the students by some means so as to cause pain as a method of punishment. Some instructors, particularly the traditional instructors arriving from the Orient, believe in maintaining discipline through the use of a swat on the back of the thighs with a stick. The author has trained in such a class and found the students' discipline to be quite strong. The contemplation of pain is a strong motivator to maintain one's self-discipline. Unfortunately, some states have laws against the use of corporal punishment making such a means of punishment a misdemeanor. It is suggested to those instructors using the "swat" method that they switch to having the students do push-ups. The author has found that 50 push-ups is as effective for discipline as is a good swat on the rear.

Individual Student Discipline

Generally maintaining class discipline is not difficult for an experienced instructor. And usually any discipline problems originate with just a few students who lack self-discipline and consequently have a difficult time maintaining their discipline in class. Unfortunately in a martial arts class where concentration is necessary, a few disruptive students can disturb the concentration of the entire class. When concentration is absent when practicing martial arts techniques, the likelihood of injury increases.

It is recommended that instructors make every effort to maintain firm discipline in class at all times. Punishment for horseplay should be other than physical contact. Those few students with low self-discipline should be especially supervised closely as their antics are the most likely to lead to injury. Strong class and individual discipline will go far to prevent negligence suits being brought against the instructor.

SPECTATORS

Another potential source of negligence lawsuits concerns spectators both in the martial arts school and at tournaments. Whenever martial arts practicing is taking place, spectators must be kept at a safe distance for their own safety.

THE SCHOOL

Within the school, control of spectators is usually quite simple. An area with a row of chairs for visitors and a barrier of some kind will generally be adequate. A visitor or spectator should never be allowed on the training floor during classes for obvious reasons. When students are engaged in free sparring, they often are not aware of bystanders. During the height of their practice it is possible for the students' momentum to carry them into a curious onlooker. Sideline spectators at football games have been seriously injured when the momentum of the play carried several players onto the sidelines. Several such cases have resulted in negligence lawsuits and large damage awards to the injured spectators. With these precedents having been established in other athletic contests, such lawsuits are also possible in the martial arts.

TOURNAMENTS

Probably the highest risk situation which could lead to spectator injury is at tournaments. Tournaments require a building with plenty of floor area in order to accommodate the necessary number of competition areas. Frequently these sites are public school or college gymnasiums, which allow the marking off of up to 8 or 10 competition squares. Without adequate planning and precautions, such gym floors quickly become chaos with a mixture of competitors and spectators jamming the floor. Proper planning will have the competition floor roped off to allow access by competitors and officials only. Additionally, sufficient control should be maintained over the competitors so as to prevent their wandering about when competitions are taking place.

The control of both spectators and competitors at tournaments cannot be too strongly stressed. The author has refereed matches at tournaments where the gym floor was so chaotic that spectators and competitors actually walked right through active sparring matches! It could only be described as luck that no injuries resulted. Should an injury occur to an individual in such a situation, however, the tournament director and sponsor could be held liable for negligence in failing to adequately demarcate the competition areas.

An additional precaution would be the use of uniformed police officers to aid in crowd control. It is the responsibility of the tournament director to make certain that the officers (who probably will have to be hired for the tournament) understand their duties. At several of the chaotic tournaments the author has attended, at least two uniformed officers have been present, but did little to diminish the chaos. Proper planning will maintain order, provide a smoothly run tournament, and (most importantly) will spare the director and sponsors the burden of having to defend themselves against a negligence lawsuit due to needless injury to a spectator or wandering competitor.

MEDICAL

There are two aspects of medical problems which could lead to a negligence lawsuit against an instructor. First, there are medical problems which arise in the school. Second, there are frequently medical problems which arise in tournaments. In both situations, proper first aid treatment of the injury, if it is serious, is important. In other sections of the chapter, we have discussed the due care necessary in order to minimize the risk of injury to students. However, there will always be injurics occuring in any athletic activity, no matter how much care is taken both by the instructors and students. This section is concerned with the care of the injury itself.

MEDICAL HISTORY

The most obvious students prone to become injured in class or competition are those having a medical problem which might tend to become aggravated by training. Examples are bad knees (trick knees), past shoulder separations, broken bones mended with the aid of inset pins, heart attacks, and high blood pressure. It is strongly recommended that each new student be questioned as to his medical history. If he has any condition that might be aggravated by training or competing, written permission should be obtained from the student's physician before allowing him to train.

INJURY DURING CLASS

It is virtually impossible to prevent injuries in class no matter how much care is exercised by both the instructor and students. Fortunately, most injuries are minor such as bruises, finger or toe sprains, or blisters. It is, however, the serious injury which may result in a negligence lawsuit if the injured student is improperly treated. It is not the purpose of this discussion to describe proper first aid treatment for various injuries. But it is recommended that every instructor take a basic first aid course such as that offered by the Red Cross.

A student who is knocked unconscious could have suffered a fractured skull, brain concussion, or broken neck either when he was struck or when he fell to the floor. Each of these injuries is very serious and requires immediate medical treatment. However the initial movement of the student must be done with care (using proper first aid procedures) or else the injury could be further worsened. This would be fertile ground for a negligence suit.

The best legal advice is that if you have no knowledge of first aid, an unconscious student should not be moved. Medical aid should be summoned immediately.

TOURNAMENTS

Any instructor organizing or sponsoring a competition tournament should have both a physician and nurse present. Serious injuries are one of the unfortunate occurrences at tournaments.

These injuries range from bloody noses to bad sprains, broken bones, or unconsciousness due to head injury. The author has attended a tournament where no doctor was present and a very serious head injury occurred to one of the participants. The seriousness of the injury indicated that prompt medical attention was necessary, yet the tournament officials delayed summoning help so that it was more than 30 minutes before an ambulance arrived. It is this type of inadequate handling of serious injuries that can result in negligence lawsuits.

LIABILITY RELEASE FORM

It is obvious from the preceding discussion that there are a number of potential situations that might lead to a negligence suit against an instructor. Additionally, however, there are a number of cautions included in the discussion which, if conscientiously adhered to by instructors, should greatly minimize the opportunity for civil damage lawsuits to arise against an instructor. As a final suggestion, it is recommended that every student or competitor be required to fill out a liability release form prior to training in his first class or prior to entering any tournament you might sponsor.

The following release has been altered and improved by three different attorneys over a period of several years and provides strong protection for the instructor—provided that all previously mentioned precautions are followed.

Figure IV–1 gives the oldest ages by both state and sex which require a parent or guardian's signature on a liability release form. The figure also gives the youngest age at which an individual may sign a liability release as an adult.

No.__________

READ THIS APPLICATION CAREFULLY. IF YOU DO NOT UNDERSTAND ANY OF ITS CLAUSES, CONSULT LEGAL COUNSEL BEFORE SIGNING

MEMBERSHIP APPLICATION

Business Phone:______________

Res. Phone:______________

NAME:____
(Surname) (First)

ADDRESS:____

DATE OF BIRTH:______________ HEIGHT:________ WEIGHT:________ SEX:_____

EDUCATION:____

OCCUPATION:______________________ EMPLOYER:______________________

MEDICAL HISTORY:____

I hereby make application for membership in (school name) and upon acceptance I sincerely pledge to obey all the rules and regulations which are set up for the purpose of keeping the order of this association and for the protection of pupils from injury. I recognize that a risk is involved in this art that requires my adherence to these rules and to the instructor's discipline.

I understand that if my application for membership is accepted, either orally or in writing by (school name) then I acknowledge and hereby release and hold harmless the Association, its officers, shareholders, Board of Directors, instructors, members, employees, servants and agents and its duly authorized and invited guests or observers from any and all claim for injury to property or to persons, which I may receive while participating in the activities of (school name) and in specific, but not by way of limitation, for the following circumstances:

1. Accidental or intentional injury by any student, instructor, guest, observer, officer, shareholder, or members of the Board of Directors of (school name):

2. Injury which may occur while in the course of training. For the purpose of this subparagraph the term "in the course of training" shall be deemed to imply any period of time which encompasses travelling to or from any training room, place of instruction, place of competition, or place of observation and shall also include self-training or with others when said training occurs outside of the premises of, or supervision of, an instructor of the (school name), or at events other than the regular or designated places of instructions. It is also understood that the aforesaid "in the course of training" shall also include any injuries suffered enroute to a function conducted by the (school name) and from said function to the individuals place of residence or business:

3. For the purpose of this release and hold harmless agreement, the term injury shall include any damage done to persons or property as a result of the activities of the (school name), whether or not said injuries are immediately apparent upon its occurrence:

4. The applicant herein represents that he or she is of lawful age to execute this release and hold harmless agreement and should the applicant not be of lawful age, the parent or guardian's signature shall be required before it shall be considered that the (school name) has accepted the application of the applicant and that said hold harmless agreement shall apply to and be binding upon said parent or legal guardian where applicable.

The applicant, and/or the applicant's parents or legal guardians hereby agree that said hold harmless agreement shall extend to all claims for injury as aforesaid, including costs of litigation, attorneys fees and other incidental expenses incurred by the (school name) in the defense of any lawsuit or to enforce this hold harmless agreement.

THE APPLICANT HAS BEEN MADE AWARE THAT THE PRACTICE OF (NAME OF THE ART) INVOLVES THE RISK OF INJURY AND AGREES TO FOLLOW THE DIRECTIONS OF THE INSTRUCTORS OF (NAME OF THE ART) SO AS TO MINIMIZE SAID RISK OF INJURIES.

DATE ____________________

____
(APPLICANT'S SIGNATURE)

IN THE PRESENCE OF:

____
(PARENT OR GUARDIAN'S SIGNATURE)

____

____

ACCEPTED: ____________________
(INSTRUCTOR)

FIGURE IV–1

Age Required to Sign Liability Release

	State	Oldest age of minor at which parent or guardian must co-sign a liability release		Youngest age at which an individual may sign a liability release as an adult	
		Male	Female	Male	Female
1.	Alabama	20[(1)]	20[(1)]	21	21
2.	Alaska	18	18	19	19
3.	Arizona	17	17	18	18
4.	Arkansas	20	17	21	18
5.	California	17	17	18	18
6.	Colorado	20	20	21	21
7.	Connecticut	17	17	18	18
8.	Delaware	17	17	18	18
9.	D.C.	20	20	21	21
10.	Florida	20[(2)]	20[(2)]	21	21
11.	Georgia	17	17	18	18
12.	Hawaii	17	17	18	18
13.	Idaho	17	17	18	18
14.	Illinois	17	17	18	18
15.	Indiana	20	20	21	21
16.	Iowa	18[(3)]	18[(3)]	19	19
17.	Kansas	17	17	18	18
18.	Kentucky	17	17	18	18
19.	Louisiana	17	17	18	18
20.	Maine	17[(4)]	17[(4)]	18	18
21.	Maryland	20	20	21	21
22.	Massachusetts	20	20	21	21
23.	Michigan	17	17	18	18
24.	Minnesota	20	20	21	21
25.	Mississippi	20	20	21	21
26.	Missouri	20	20	21	21
27.	Montana	17	17	18	18
28.	Nebraska	18[(5)]	18[(5)]	19	19
29.	Nevada	20	17	21	18
30.	New Hampshire	20	20	21	21
31.	New Jersey	17	17	18	18
32.	New Mexico	17	17	18	18
33.	New York	20[(6)]	20[(6)]	21	21
34.	North Carolina	17	17	18	18
35.	North Dakota	17	17	18	18
36.	Ohio	20	17	21	18
37.	Oklahoma	17	17	18	18

38.	Oregon	20[7]	20[7]	21	21
39.	Pennsylvania	17	17	18	18
40.	Rhode Island	17	17	18	18
41.	South Carolina	20	20	21	21
42.	South Dakota	20	17	21	18
43.	Tennessee	17	17	18	18
44.	Texas	20[8]	20[8]	21	21
45.	Utah	20	17	21	18
46.	Vermont	17	17	18	18
47.	Virginia	17	17	18	18
48.	Washington	17	17	18	18
49.	West Virginia	17	17	18	18
50.	Wisconsin	17	17	18	18
51.	Wyoming	20	20	21	21

NOTES:

1.	Alabama	18, if married
2.	Florida	any age if married
3.	Iowa	any age if married
4.	Maine	any age if married
5.	Nebraska	any age if married
6.	New York	any age if married
7.	Oregon	any age if married
8.	Texas	any age if married

Part V

SELECTING A LAWYER

Chapter 12

SELECTING A LAWYER

This text has dealt entirely with the legal problems students and instructors of the martial arts may become entangled in when either using or instructing defense techniques. Therefore, it is certainly appropriate to conclude the book with a chapter on how to go about finding a lawyer if the need arises. As has been pointed out earlier, this book cannot replace the expertise of an attorney if you need to appear in a court of law. However, it is the intent of the book to provide you with the knowledge as to the various possibilities which might bring you to court and then what procedures to expect once you are in court. It is obvious that no one wishes to have to appear in court to defend himself against criminal or civil charges. If you must go to court, then by all means obtain the advice and assistance of a lawyer as soon as possible. To delay obtaining an attorney's services in order to save yourself a few dollars will probably be somewhat more expensive in terms of money and time in the long run than your initial savings.

THE FUNCTIONS OF A LAWYER

What will a lawyer do for you? There are a number of functions which an attorney will perform for you. These include (but are not limited to):

1. Business formation (for new schools).
2. Liability release preparation.
3. Civil trial preparation and defense.
4. Criminal trial preparation and defense.
5. Appellate court trial preparation and defense.

Just as professionals in fields other than law (medicine, engineering, teachers) tend to specialize, so do lawyers. Consequently, there are criminal lawyers, trial lawyers, tort lawyers, tax attorneys, appellate attorneys, patent and copyright lawyers, and real estate lawyers. Additionally, just as there are general practitioner doctors (the family physician), there are lawyers who handle a number of general legal problems (such as house and real estate titles, wills) not requiring in-depth specialization.

If you are starting a new self-defense school and/or preparing a new liability release form for your school or tournament, a general lawyer can be most adequate. On the other hand, if you receive a summons and complaint for a negligence suit being brought against you, then a civil (or tort) trial attorney would be better able to help you. Likewise a criminal trial attorney would be necessary to defend you in criminal court. If you proceed through a civil or criminal trial and lose but wish to appeal the decision, then you may choose an appellate court attorney (one specializing in appeal cases) to present your case. Your previous trial attorney, however, may also be quite capable of handling your appeal.

WHERE TO FIND A LAWYER

When faced with a legal problem of a serious nature, such as criminal charges or civil lawsuit, it will be wise to select your legal representative with care. The following sources can guide you to a competent lawyer:

1. Friends who themselves have had legal problems which required an attorney.

2. Attorneys where you work can make suggestions.
3. The Martindale-Hubbel Law Directory which is a geographical listing of all U.S. attorneys and provides a simple rating system for each. This source can be found in any public library.

PAYING A LAWYER

Following this process of gathering suggestions, you can next investigate the costs involved. Generally, within an area, lawyers tend to charge the same fees for equivalent services. There are however, several methods through which attorneys charge for their services: set rate, by the hour, by the day, and by percentage of the recovery.

Within the context we are discussing, you will probably not encounter a set rate payment charge. This might more aptly pertain to drawing up wills or handling real estate titles. In defending you against criminal charges or civil lawsuit, payment will probably be on a time basis, either hourly or daily. To these time charges, the attorney will also add nontime related expenses such as postage, long distance phone calls, travel expenses, stenographic services, and document fees. In the author's area of New Jersey, lawyers charge $50 or more hourly for their services. If you are seeking to recover damages from another person for injuries he caused you, then the attorney may be willing to represent you for a percent of the court awarded compensation. The percent can range from 25% up to as high as 50% depending on the amount recovered.

WORKING RELATIONSHIP

Throughout the duration of your legal problem, it is important to maintain a good working relationship with your attorney. If a severe conflict occurs between you and your lawyer, it is possible to dismiss him and obtain another lawyer. However, you will be obligated to compensate the attorney for his services up to the time of his dismissal. This is obviously a costly thing to do. For this reason, before you agree to accept an attorney's services, you should have a complete understanding of his capability to competently and diligently handle your case, how (in general) he will proceed and how he will charge you for his services. You should also inquire about what nontime related expenses he will charge you for. During this initial fact-finding and understanding discussion, you can also determine the compatibility of your personalities. A well-chosen attorney will be well worth your initial search efforts.

GLOSSARY

ACCIDENT. A person does not want a certain outcome to occur and even though he is reasonably careful, the outcome occurs anyway.

APPEAL. Attempt by a defense attorney to get a higher appellate court to reverse the decision of a lower court which has found his client guilty.

ARRAIGNMENT. Process whereby the person indicted by a grand jury is brought before the court and fully advised of the charges against him.

ARREST. The act of taking some individual into legal custody with the intent that he be charged with having violated some law.

ASSAULT (SIMPLE). An unlawful apparent attempt, by a person having the apparent ability, to commit bodily injury on another person.

BAIL. A financial guarantee made by the accused and deposited with the court providing some assurance that the accused will return to the court on an appointed date.

BATTERY. Unlawful contact made on a person by a voluntary physical act of the aggressor against the consent of the victim.

CIVIL LAW. Roman civil law was a highly organized body of law developed in the Roman Empire long before common law originated. See TORT.

CODE. A collection of state or federal statutes or city ordinances.

COMMON LAW. Early body of law, originating in England from customs. First organized body of law in the U.S.

COMMUTATION. Reduction of prison term by order of the President of the United States or by a state governor.

CORONER'S JURY. Evaluates evidence concerning homicides to determine if a crime has been committed and by whom.

CRIME. A wrong committed against a state or the United States which violates a specific law and is punishable by a fine and/or imprisonment or jail sentence.

CROSS-EXAMINATION. The right of an attorney in a trial to question the opposing attorney's witnesses about any subjects on which the witness has testified.

DAMAGES. Monetary compensation which a civil court requires a defendant to pay for injuries or harm he has wrongfully done to another person.

DEADLY WEAPON. Any object which is used to cause serious bodily injury or death.

DEFENDANT. The alleged or accused committer of a crime or tort.

FELONY. A serious crime such as murder, robbery, arson or rape and which is tried in a state or federal court and is punished with either death or a prison term.

GAULT CASE. 1966 U.S. Supreme Court case, the decision of which substantially strengthened the Constitutional rights of juveniles who have been arrested.

GIDEON V. WAINWRIGHT. A 1963 U.S. Supreme Court decision which guarantees that every accused person brought before a court is entitled to legal counsel. If he cannot afford to hire his own attorney, one must be provided at taxpayers' expense.

GRAND JURY. A jury that decides if a sufficient level of evidence exists sufficient to establish a reasonable belief that the accused committed a crime. Usually 23 members 12 votes required to charge the accused. Not a trial jury.

HABEAS CORPUS. A demand by the court for a defendant to be produced in person by whomever is holding him in custody and either file a specific charge against or release him.

HOMICIDE. The killing of one human being by another. Criminal homicide is either murder or manslaughter. Noncriminal homicides are killings which the law will not prosecute because no guilt is placed on the killer, categorized into justifiable and excusable.

INDICTMENT. Charged with a crime as a result of the findings of a grand jury.

INTENT. A state of mind whereby a person wants a certain outcome to occur.

JUDGE. Interprets the law for the jury in a trial as the law pertains to that case.

JURY. A group of citizens (usually 12) assembled to determine the facts in a criminal or civil case. Three kinds are petit, grand, and coroner's juries.

LAW. A rule of human conduct or action which either has been established by custom or else has been legislated into being by an authorized group.

LOCO PARENTIS. Acting as a substitute for a child's parents.

MAIMING. The act of permanently crippling or disfiguring an opponent in a fight.

MANSLAUGHTER. Criminal homicide which is not premeditated and categorized as either voluntary or involuntary. (Voluntary) Commits homicide while under the influence of excessively strong emotions. (Involuntary) Unintended or unpremeditated homicide committed while engaged in an unlawful act less serious than a felony.

MALICE. Premediated intent to commit a crime such as murder. Same as malice aforethought.

MALICE AFORETHOUGHT. See malice.

MAYHEM. The crime of maiming (see definition).

MENS REA. Intent to commit a crime.

MIRANDA V. ARIZONA. A 1966 U.S. Supreme Court decision which requires that arresting police officers warn suspects of their Constitutional rights.

MISDEMEANOR. An illegal act less serious than a felony and which is tried in a county or municipal court and which is punished with a fine and/or a jail sentence.

MURDER. Any premeditated or intentional illegal killing of a person; criminal homicide. First degree murder is homicide with expressed malice, making intent known beforehand.

Second degree murder is homicide with implied malice, intent deduced from actions.

Felony murder is criminal homicide which occurs during the commission of a felony.

NEGLIGENCE. Utter and complete disregard for the safety and health of others. An act which an average reasonable and prudent person would not commit.

NO BILL. A grand jury ruling that insufficient evidence exists to charge an accused person with having committed a crime.

NUNCHAKU. Weapon consisting of 2 sticks (about 12 inches long and 1-inch thick each) connected by a chain or rope about 6–12 inches long.

ORDINANCE. A law enacted by a city.

PARDON. Permanent freedom from a sentence granted by either a state governor or the U.S. President.

PAROLE. A probationary release which may be granted to a convicted person after he has served a specified minimum prison term.

PETITION. A document filed in juvenile court identifying a youthful offender and specifying his offense. Equivalent to an "indictment" filed in adult criminal court or a "complaint" filed in adult civil court.

PETIT JURY. The primary trial jury for criminal and civil cases. Consists of 12 jurors (may be only 6 in some municipal courts).

PLAINTIFF. The victim of a crime or a tort.

PRECEDENT. The principle of stare decisis (or the doctrine of precedent) is a characteristic of English common law whereby the written decisions of each case are accumulated and the courts tend to follow the principles decided in previous cases.

SELF-DEFENSE. Any person fearing death or serious bodily harm from the assault and/or battery of an attacker has the legal right to defend himself using a reasonable amount of force, but may kill the attacker only if necessary to save his own life.

STATUTE. A law enacted by either a federal or state legislative governmental body.

SUMMONS. A court order demanding that a defendant answer a civil complaint which has been brought against him in the court.

TEXAS RULE. The majority of states view on retreating when attacked—an individual who is not a trespasser, need not retreat from an assailant if he (the defender) truly fears death or serious bodily harm.

TORT. A wrong committed against an individual punished by requiring payment of damages to the injured person. Falls under modern civil law (as opposed to ancient Roman Civil law).

TRUE BILL. A grand jury indictment against a person accused of committing a crime.

U.S. CONSTITUTION. The highest governing law in the U.S. taking precedence over all state laws and city ordinances.

WARRANT. A written document issued by a court ordering the arrest of a specified person.

BIBLIOGRAPHY

American Jurisprudence 2nd ed., V. 6 Assault and Battery, 1963, pp. 1–180; V. 21 Crime, 1965, pp. 65–574; V. 22 Damages, 1965, 1–552; V. 40 Homicide, 1968, 277–848; V. 57, Negligence 1971, 317–887; V. 58, Negligence 1971, 1–125; V. 74 Torts, 1974, 613–696; V. 75 Trial, 1974, 81–872; V. 76 Trial, 1975; 1–220; V. 79 Weapons, 1975, 1–52. The Lawyers Co-operative Publishing Company, Rochester, New York.

Appenzeller, Herb, 1970—*From the Gym to the Jury*, The Michie Company, Charlottesville, Virginia, 221 pp.

Asch, Sidney H., 1967—*Police Authority and the Rights of the Individual*, Arco Publishing Company, Inc., New York, 126 pp.

Baum, Frederic S, and Baum, Joan 1970—*Law of Self-Defense*, Oceana Publications, Inc. Dobbs Ferry, New York, 123 pp.

Casper, Jonathan D., 1972—*American Criminal Justice, The Defendant's Perspective*, Prentice-Hall, Inc., Englewood Cliffs, New Jersey, 178 pp.

Coughlin, George G., 1975—*Your Introduction to Law*, Barnes & Noble, Inc., New York 310 pp.

Coulsan, Robert 1968—*How to Stay Out of Court*, Crown Publishers, Inc., New York, 224 pp.

Deming, Richard, 1970—*Man And Society—Criminal Law at Work*, Hawthorn Books, Inc., New York, 180 pp.

Deming, Richard 1972—*Man Against Man, Civil Law at Work*, Hawthorn Books, Inc., New York, 210 pp.

Farmer, Robert A., 1967—*Crime, the Law and You*, Arco Publishing Company, Inc., New York, 126 pp.

Farmer, Robert A., 1967—*How to Collect on Peronal Injuries*, Arco Publishing Co., Inc., New York, 104 pp.

Fellman, David, 1958—*The Defendant's Rights*, Rinehart & Company, Inc., New York, 356 pp.

Fox, Sanford J., 1970—*The Law of Juvenile Courts in a Nutshell*, West Publishing Co., St. Paul, Minnesota.

Frankel, Marvin E., 1973—*Criminal Sentences*, Hill and Wang, New York, 124 pp.

Friedman, Lawrence M., 1973—*A History of American Law*, Simon and Schuster, New York, 655 pp.

Gammage, Allen Z., and Hemphill, Charles F. Jr., 1974—*Basic Criminal Law*, McGraw-Hill Book Company, New York, 333 pp.

Gatti, Daniel J. and Richard D., 1972, *The Teacher and the Law,* Parker Publishing Company, Inc., West Nyack, New York, 206 pp.
Gifis, Steven, H., 1975—*Law Dictionary,* Barron's Educational Series, Inc., Woodbury, New York, 227 pp.
Hahn, Paul H., 1971, *The Juvenile Offender and the Law,* The W.H. Anderson Company, Cincinnati, Ohio.
Helm, Alice K, (ed.) 1974, *The Family Legal Adviser,* Greystone Press, New York, 480 pp.
Imbau, Fred E. and Aspen, Marvin E., 1970—*Criminal Law for the Layman,* Chilton Book Company, Radnor, Pennsylvania, 190 pp.
Kalven, Harry, Jr. and Zeisel, Hans, 1966—*The American Jury,* Little, Brown, Boston, Massachusetts.
LaSalle Law Library, 1965—Vol. 2 Torts; Vol. 3 Criminal Law and Procedure, Vol. 10 Attachment and Garnishment, Vol. 11 Pleading, LaSalle Extension University, Chicago, Illinois.
Lehman, Godfrey, 1968—*What You Need to Know for Jury Duty,* Cowles Education Corporation, New York, 181 pp.
Lieberman, Jethro K., 1966—*Court in Session,* Sterling Publishing Co., Inc., New York, 112 pp.
McCart, Samuel W., 1964—*Trial By Jury,* Chilton Books, New York 204 pp.
Moreland, Roy 1952—*The Law of Homicide,* The Bobbs-Merrill Company, Inc., Indianapolis, Indiana, 338 pp.
Parker, Frank J., 1972—*The Law and the Poor,* Orbis Books, Maryknoll, New York, 218 pp.
Perkins, Rollin M., 1969—*Perkins on Criminal Law,* Foundation Press, Mineola, N.Y.
Raphael, Jesse S., 1962—*The Collier Quick and Easy Guide to Law,* Collier Books, New York, N.Y. 160 pp.
Reader's Digest 1971—*You and the Law,* The Reader's Digest Association, Inc., Pleasantville, New York, 863 pp.
Rich, Vernon 1975—*Law and the Administration of Justice,* John Wiley & Sons, Inc., New York, 417 pp.
Rosett, Arthur and Cressey, Donald R., 1976—*Justice By Consent,* J. B. Lippincott Company, New York, 227 pp.
Ross, Martin, I., 1967, *Handbook of Everyday Law,* Fawcett Publications, Inc., Greenwich, Connecticut, 335 pp.
Shain, Henry, 1975, *Legal First Aid,* Funk & Wagnalls, New York, 366 pp.
Wehringer, Cameron K., 1970, *When and How to Choose an Attorney,* Oceana Publications, Inc., Dobbs Ferry, New York, 120 pp.
Weinreb, Lloyd L., 1969—*Criminal Law,* Foundation Press, Mineola, New York.
Wormser, Rene A., 1962—*The Story of the Law,* Simon and Schuster, New York, 606 pp.
Zarr, Melvyn, 1970—*The Bill of Rights and the Police,* Oceana Publications, Inc., Dobbs Ferry, New York, 119 pp.

INDEX